JOHN A. HARRISON

a woman

ALONE

Mona Bell, Sam Hill, and the
Mansion on Bonneville Rock

Frank
Amato
PORTLAND

JOHN A. HARRISON lives in Vancouver, Washington, where he was a reporter at *The Columbian* newspaper in the 1980s. For several years his beat included the Columbia River Gorge. Having read about Mona Bell in a biography of Sam Hill, John decided to look for the mansion that Sam built for Mona in 1928. He found it—or, more precisely its remains—on an overgrown hill overlooking Bonneville Dam.

Intrigued, John decided to write Mona's story. He found people in the Portland, Oregon/Vancouver, Washington area who worked on the construction of Bonneville Dam in the 1930s and who, surprisingly, had strong memories of the controversial Mona even after 50 years. The story launched John on a search to find out more about this mystery woman of the Gorge, her relationship with Sam Hill, and what happened to her.

Today John is the Information Officer at the Northwest Power and Conservation Council, a Portland-based regional energy-planning agency. He is the author of an almanac-style history of the Columbia River that is posted on the Council's website at www.nwcouncil.org/history. He has a bachelor's degree in communications from Washington State University and a master's degree in journalism from the University of Oregon. John and his wife, Dawn, are the parents of two grown sons. For more information about Mona Bell Hill, including photographs, maps, and documents, visit jharrisononline.com.

Published in 2009 by Frank Amato Publications, Inc.
P.O. Box 82112, Portland, Oregon 97282
(503) 653-8108

Book design: Craig Wann
Cover design: Tony Amato
Title Page design: John C. Harrison www.blueskyhill.com
Title Page photo: Library of Congress, Prints and Photographs Division, Historic American Engineering Record, Reproduction No. HAER OR-36-0-10.

Excerpts from *The Bonneville Dream*, copyright 1991 by Lorena S. Fisher; *Maryhill, Sam Hill, and Me*, copyright 1978, Lois David Plotts; and *Sam Hill, Prince of Castle Nowhere*, copyright 1983, John E. Tuhy, used with permission.

ISBN-10: 1-57188-452-1 • ISBN-13: 978-1-57188-452-7
UPC: 0-81127-00288-7

Printed in Singapore   **51178135**

10 9 8 7 6 5 4 3 2 1

contents

INTRODUCTION

In Search of Mona Bell Hill

ORTY MILES EAST OF DOWNTOWN PORTLAND, OREGON, ON THE SUMMIT OF A HILL SOME 200 FEET ABOVE THE COLUMBIA RIVER AND BONNEVILLE DAM, LIE THE REMAINS OF ONE OF THE MOST MAGNIFICENT STRUCTURES ever built in the Columbia River Gorge: the 20-room mansion of Edith Mona Bell Hill. There among the tall Douglas firs, nearly hidden under overgrown bushes, blackberry vines and the occasional poison oak bush, lie the toppled remains of a massive chimney, a red, stamped-concrete terrace, pieces of the foundation, and steps that led to the front door of the mansion.

The hill today is truncated and uninviting, its southern and northern flanks cut away for busy Interstate 84 on the south and the Union Pacific Railroad tracks on the north. But in the 1930s, the old Columbia River Highway looped around the south side of the hill and the Oregon-Washington Railroad and Navigation Company tracks curved along the river shore on the north side. Mona's mansion commanded the hilltop, where she landscaped more than an acre with plants from as far away as Japan and India. In all, she owned 34 acres. It was an estate that the Governor of Oregon, Julius Meyer, described in 1934 as even more spectacular than his own substantial estate, Menucha, 18 miles to the west.

And yet today there is virtually no trace of the estate and no marker to note its existence. There is only a locked gate at the top of the off-ramp from Interstate 84 westbound to Bonneville Dam and an overgrown access path up the east side of the hill that apparently is rarely used. Directly across Interstate 84 to the south, informational signs at the Tooth Rock Trailhead describe the historic highway and Tooth Rock. But there is nothing about Mona, whose hill rises abruptly on the other side of the noisy freeway.

Who was this woman, and how did she come to own such a showplace? How long did she live there, when and why did she leave? Where did she go? Why is the mansion no longer standing?

These questions captured my attention more than 20 years ago and did not let go. I have a strong interest in Northwest history. I first learned about Mona in 1985 when I read John Tuhy's biography of Sam Hill.[1]   Sam, the son-in-law of railroader James J. Hill (it was a coincidence they had the same last name), was an early 20th century Northwest entrepreneur, philanthropist, and tireless promoter of good roads. He built the Maryhill Museum and the Stonehenge war memorial farther east in the Columbia River Gorge, and also the Peace Arch on the Washington/British Columbia border beside present-day Interstate 5.

Tuhy wrote briefly about Mona, one of Sam Hill's three known mistresses, noting that she met him in 1910 in Grand Forks, North Dakota, where Mona worked. Tuhy recounts some stories about Mona that her son told him—that she had performed in a wild-West show, was a crack shot, and had been a world traveler, including a solo safari in Africa in the 1930s. I read that Sam Hill, 33 years her senior, built the mansion in the Gorge for Mona and was the father of her son, born in Portland in 1928. She named him Sam, after his father. Tuhy also wrote that the home and acreage was condemned by the federal government to make way for Bonneville Dam, that Mona and her son were evicted, and that the home ultimately was demolished.

I was a reporter for *The Columbian* newspaper in Vancouver, Washington. Part of my beat included covering the Columbia River Gorge. I knew the area around Bonneville Dam well. I was intrigued, and so I decided to try to find the hilltop and write about the mansion and Mona. I wondered whether she still were alive. I wondered what had happened to Mona's son. Tuhy obviously had talked to him. Where was he?

I asked a few old-timers who had lived at Bonneville at the time the dam was built whether they remembered Mona. Oh, yes, they said. They remembered her son, too, who lived with her on the hilltop. They described Mona as friendly but also aloof, imperious, and mysterious, a woman who had little to do with others in the community, and her son as handsome but sad and apparently quite lonely. They said it was widely rumored, but never confirmed by Mona, that Sam Hill built the mansion for her and was the father of her child. One said, "he looked just like Sam."

Finding the hill was easy. It is immediately south of the navigation lock at the dam. A *Columbian* photographer and I tramped around the hilltop. We saw the toppled remains of the chimney, the steps, part of a foundation wall with decorative swirls trowled into the concrete, and a small section of a patio, painted red and neatly scored in a pattern of rectangles. We also found bushes of the kind usually planted around homes—low-growing arbor vitae and some more exotic flowering bushes that we did not recognize. Pink rhododendrons still bloom on the hilltop in the spring.

With Tuhy's help I contacted Sam Bettle Hill, who at the time was 58 years old and living in Venice, California, where he worked as a psychotherapist. I called him and explained that I would like to write a story about his mother, the missing mansion, and his memories of her and his boyhood home above the Columbia River. He agreed and said he planned to be in the Portland area soon. We arranged to meet.

A few weeks later, in October, I met Sam.[2] We hit it off right away. I found him gregarious, funny, profane, easy to talk to, and full of memories of his mother. I was sorry to learn that she had died just four years earlier, and I told him so. Curiously, I thought, he seemed almost dismissive about her death—certainly more relieved than saddened, I thought.

He talked and talked; I listened. I took notes and wrote the article. He liked it, and partly because of that and partly because I thought Mona's story was so interesting, I proposed that we collaborate on a book about her.

He seemed interested and said he would consider it.

Two months later, in December 1985, I received a letter. In scrawling handwriting on a sheet of yellow paper from a legal pad, Sam poured out his stream-of-consciousness thoughts about my proposal:

> *A book about my mother—that is one hell of an idea!*
> *I'm sitting on my bed at the ridiculous time of 3 a.m., either unable to sleep or not willing to—the predominant thought that runs through my mind is that neither of us could adequately represent her essence with words—more than even my father, she was bigger than life. She lived 92 years and at least seven decades of that long life was spent in an intensity that I could never really reduce to some process of conceptualization—as her son I mostly 'reacted' and infrequently responded.*

Yet in ways I am joyously like my mother. God only knows the composition of her ESSENCE. On the outside life was a performance—the world was (in my case!) here to poke at, laugh at, and, yes, occasionally violate. Behind her sound and fury I think she was secretly smiling at the whole damn play! Mona Bell Hill had an impact on almost everyone who knew her, more often negative than positive, perhaps. I don't know for sure. The way I am like her, John, is that I like to live my life alternating between hero and asshole.

John, I accept your proposition with a mite of trepidation and a grand dose of excitement.

Hell, let's do it!

—Sam Hill

That was the last I ever heard from him.

It was 1985, long before the Internet and e-mail. I had only the telephone and the regular mail to reach him, and neither was successful. The return address on his letter was a post office box in Lancaster, California, and so evidently he had moved. I tried telephone directories and city directories for Venice and Lancaster. I tried local business associations and newspapers, hoping someone might know him. No luck. I sent a letter to the Lancaster post office box, but it was returned as undeliverable. His phone was disconnected. I decided not to look for him in person unless I knew where to look, and I really didn't know where he was.

Years passed.

From time to time I went back to my notes and tried again to find Sam or his relatives, but to no avail—no published telephone number, no forwarding address, no one who remembered him. I didn't stop looking into Mona's life, either. I researched her past, including Sam's claims that she traveled the world, performed in a wild-West show, and had worked as a newspaper reporter. I researched public records about the mansion and how Mona came to own it, and also federal court records in the national archives in Seattle. But I still could not find Sam, and tracing Mona proved much more difficult than I anticipated. Both seemed to have simply disappeared.

Then, in 2007, when I took up the search yet again, I had a breakthrough: the telephone number of Sam's ex-wife, Virginia. Until that moment I had not known her name. For reasons I did not understand in 1985, Sam would not tell me.

I felt as if I had been handed a gold nugget from a stream I had panned repeatedly in the past.

CHAPTER 1

Mona Bell

"I want people to know about my mother."
— *Samuel Bettle Hill*

EDITH MONA BELL WAS BORN JANUARY 13, 1890, IN EAST GRAND FORKS, MINNESOTA, AN EASTERN SUBURB OF GRAND FORKS, NORTH DAKOTA. SHE WAS ONE OF THREE CHILDREN OF ESTHER M. MOLSON AND HENRY H. Bell. The Bells owned a grocery store, which Esther ran most of the time because Henry traveled for his job building grain silos. Mona later would tell her son that her father was an alcoholic and, when home, frequently was drunk.

Mona always was tall for her age, and she grew into a tall woman—five feet seven or eight inches. She was athletic and coordinated, and she enjoyed being outdoors. She learned to ride horses and to shoot rifles and pistols accurately.

She left home at the age of 18 and enrolled at the University of North Dakota in Grand Forks. She was a student there in the fall, winter, and spring terms of 1907-08, and for part of the fall term of 1908. Her classes included pedagogy (education), botany, geometry, German, political economics, English, and chemistry. She listed her home address as the family residence in East Grand Forks. She did not declare a major and did not earn a degree.[3] She also played basketball, something her official records do not indicate. This was the extent of her formal education. She did not enroll in college again.

It is not clear today why Mona left the university, but it may have been to join a wild-West show. Sam B. Hill said his mother told him she performed as a bareback rider and trick shooter—rather like Annie Oakley, who was a star for arguably the most famous of the wild-West shows, Buffalo Bill's Wild West. The Wild West performed in three central Minnesota cities in August 1908—the first time back in the state since 1902—in five southern Minnesota cities in August 1909, and in Grand Forks, up north, on August 24, 1910.

Mona claimed to have performed in Buffalo Bill's show, but that appears unlikely for several reasons. First, Bill Cody was a traditionalist, and while women were participating in wild west shows by the mid-1890s as bronc riders, steer riders, fancy ropers, bulldoggers, and even performing the crowd-pleasing "diving horse" trick, Bill Cody's show was more like a rodeo and he did not employ very many specialists. He did have female performers, but many of them rode side-saddle. Second, there is no record today of Mona ever being on the payroll for the Wild West, which by 1907-08 was waning. The show was hugely popular when it debuted in 1883, but by the time the show was sold in a bankruptcy auction in Denver in 1913 dozens of imitators had come and gone, saturating the market for that type of entertainment. In fact, between 1883 and the early 1940s, when wild-West shows faded into history, there had been at least 115. The fact that Mona was never on Bill Cody's payroll, however, does not mean she was not an employee of the show somewhere at some time; there's just no record of it today. And third, female bareback riders were rare in wild-West shows. The first record of a woman riding bareback was in 1916 at a wild-West show in Chicago.[4]

Nonetheless, Mona did compete in rodeos. Dressed as a man, she rode broncos, her son said. Mona knew she was attractive, and once won a bet with a couple of North Dakota cowboys. It was 1909, and she was 19 years old.

"Mother's Day was coming up, and this guy told her she wasn't very pretty," Sam B. Hill said. "So she made him a bet that she could pretty herself up and that she would have a photo taken to prove it. The bet was on. She rented a necklace for 5 cents, a flower for 5 cents, and a dress. She had the picture taken, and then she showed the guy and said, 'you're going to pay.' He paid. He had to admit she was a real fox."

By the next year, 1910, Mona had traded the cowgirl life for a sit-down job as a newspaper reporter in Grand Forks. She covered the city's society, as well as what then was widely called "women's news"—fashion, homemaking, cooking. She chafed at it, as she always would regarding what she considered "women's work," but it was a job, and she enjoyed the exhilaration of being a reporter, even on the society beat, her son said.

Mona met Sam Hill in Grand Forks that year, beginning a relationship that would last until his death 21 years later. One version of how they met is that he sought her out after seeing her perform with Buffalo Bill's Wild West, which performed in Grand Forks on August 24, 1910. However, this is unlikely because a letter among Sam's correspondence in the archives at Maryhill Museum shows he was in Seattle on August 23—one day before the Wild West performed in Grand Forks—when he wrote to Charles H. Babcock, a long-time friend and former associate at the Great Northern Railway, that he had just returned home from the second International Road Congress, which was held in Brussels from July 31 to August 7. The more likely version of how Mona met Sam—the version told by her son, in fact—is that Sam gave a speech in Grand Forks—possibly on his way back to Seattle from the Road Congress—and that Mona covered the social aspects of the event for the newspaper. There is some support for this version in the fact that the following month, September 1910, Sam wrote to his niece that he was busy with his work promoting good roads. Precisely when he spoke in Grand Forks, however, is not clear.

Though 33 years apart in age, Mona and Sam had an instant rapport, according to a story she told her son. According to the story, as they talked, Mona mentioned her interests, including horses and basketball, and Sam commented on her height and apparent strength. At this, she bet him she could lift Sam off the ground—a dare, probably, as he invited her to try. And she did—wrapped her arms around him and lifted him off the floor. He was impressed, and told her so. He gave her a ride home that evening. Having learned her birthday, after that he never failed to send her a card. Over the ensuing years, they kept in periodic contact by letter. They may or may not have traveled together. There is no record of it, but Sam B. Hill thought it was likely, especially on his father's periodic international trips.

Mona and Sam would become close in the 1920s, when Mona moved to Portland, where Sam was splitting his time with his home in Seattle. What did she see in him, a man clearly old enough to be her father—a suggestive fact in its own right?

"Sam was very debonair, and Mona was captivated by him," Mona's daughter-in-law, Virginia Hill, said.[5] "She had a strong personality, and so did he. Mona Bell was very strong-minded, and he evidently liked that in her. I think she really liked who he was."

Mona did not stay long in Grand Forks after meeting Sam in 1910. According to her son, she moved to New York City where she worked for a company that produced advertising placards for street cars, and then crossed the country working for newspapers.

"My mother always was proud of being a reporter," Sam B. Hill said. "She worked for about 25 papers; God knows where they all were."

Minneapolis, Omaha, El Paso, San Francisco, Portland (Oregon)—all are possible stops in Mona's journalism career, according to family stories, but there is no proof of it today—no surviving articles with bylines, and no employment records, for example. Wherever she lived, she apparently kept her personal life personal, for the most part. She married twice; each ended in divorce. There are no surviving details of one of the marriages, and only a little about the other. Mona's relatives don't remember the man's name, but he was a dentist. The marriage was short—Mona's sister, Frances, convinced her to divorce the man or annul the marriage. He was the father of the only other child Mona conceived, a girl who was stillborn. Apparently, the dentist had something to do with the birth—or maybe he was just a bad dentist—because Mona usually referred to him as "The Butcher."

CHAPTER 2

Sam Hill

*T*HE QUIRKY AND COLORFUL SAM HILL, RAILROADER, VISIONARY ENTREPRENEUR AND TIRELESS PROMOTER OF GOOD ROADS, PACIFISM, AND ART, WAS BORN MAY 13, 1857 IN DEEP RIVER, NORTH CAROLINA, near Greensboro. He was the fourth of the six children of Nathan Bronson Hill, a physician, and Eliza L. Mendenhall. They were Quakers and abolitionists, and this led to strained relations with many of their increasingly secessionist neighbors.

Refusing to endorse slavery and fearing retribution in the pro-slavery South as the Civil War broke out, Nathan and Eliza feared for their lives and the lives of their children. Like many other Quaker families in central North Carolina at the time, they left the state. Their journey was long and circuitous, first going south to Georgia to avoid suspicion from their neighbors, then north through Alabama, Tennessee, Kentucky, Indiana, and eventually Minnesota, where they settled in Minneapolis in September 1861. When he was 17, Sam got his first job for a railroad, working on a survey crew for the Lake Superior and Mississippi Road. The next year, 1875, he was one of six young men chosen by an executive of the Pennsylvania Railroad for informal instruction in matters of road and railroad construction. Many years later, Sam would tell Fred Lockley, a columnist for *The Oregon Daily Journal* newspaper in Portland, that this was the beginning of his interest in good roads.[6]

Sam entered Haverford College in Pennsylvania, his father's alma mater, in 1875 and graduated in 1878 with an AB degree[7], having studied a broad curriculum that included classical languages, mathematics, literature, and history. He entered Harvard in 1878, qualifying for entry as a senior. He spent a year, again studying a broad mix of subjects including Latin and philosophy, and graduated in 1879 with another AB degree. He returned to Minneapolis and began work at a law firm. He was tall, handsome, gregarious, well-educated and, in short, eligible. Soon he was involved in a number of local civic, political (he was a

Republican), and fraternal organizations, including the Bachelors' Club, of which he was president.[8] He also was a fine lawyer.

All of this did not go unnoticed.

Sam told Lockley that he took many personal injury cases against the Great Northern Railroad and won so often that in 1886, when he was 29, the Empire Builder himself, James J. Hill (no relation), president of the Great Northern, sent for him and told him, "We would rather have you with us than against us." From this meeting, negotiations between the two men led eventually to Sam accepting Hill's offer to be assistant counsel for his St. Paul and Pacific Railroad. It also led to an introduction to J.J.'s eldest child, his daughter Mary Frances.

James J. Hill emigrated to the United States from a small town in rural Ontario, Canada, in 1838 when he was 17 years old and soon became involved in the transportation and fuel businesses in Minnesota. He was a shrewd, prescient businessman with an innate gift for being in the right places at the right times to create or take over businesses, including several railroads, and build them into an empire of related companies that eventually stretched across the northern tier of the country. In 1878, when he was 57, he and four associates took over the St. Paul & Pacific Railroad, soon completed a connection to Saskatchewan, and by 1893 another to Seattle. By acquiring small railroads and merging them, he built the Great Northern and later took over the Burlington Railroad and the bankrupt Northern Pacific, as well. While he was one of America's wealthiest and most influential businessmen, he also was the consummate family man, equally devoted to his cross-continental business empire and to his large family.

Mary Frances Hill was born in St. Paul in 1868. In all, James and Mary Hill would have nine children. Mamie, as her parents called her, grew up with the perks of her parents' wealth—opulent homes, a private education, frequent travel, servants. As the eldest daughter of one of America's wealthiest men, she was a catch, for sure, and the man who caught her eye was the tall, handsome Sam Hill, 11 years her senior and a rising star in one of her father's railroads. Probably they met through the various social activities and groups in Minneapolis and St. Paul, and while the precise date of their engagement is unknown, probably it was in 1887.[9]

Sam and Mamie were married on Sept. 6, 1888, in her parents' mansion in St. Paul. A church service was out of the question as Mamie and her parents were Catholics and Sam had been raised a Quaker. A priest, however, officiated at the ceremony, and so it was a Catholic wedding. This fact would prove important in Sam's later life.

As a wedding gift, James J. and Mary gave the couple 1,000 shares of stock in the St. Paul, Minneapolis & Manitoba Railroad, which had been created by Hill and several associates in 1879 when they bought the interests of a bankrupt line.[10] The value of the stock was $100,000, and the annual dividend it generated amounted to $6,000. In short, it was a fortune. Adjusted for inflation through 2008, the principal was worth at least $2 million, and the annual interest more than $120,000. "This would supplement Sam's earnings nicely, to say the least," historian Albro Martin wrote in his 1976 biography of James J. Hill.[11]

Sam and Mamie left immediately on a honeymoon tour of Europe, and when they returned she was pregnant. Their first child, whom they named Mary at James J.'s suggestion, was born òn July 3, 1889. Her first name honored her mother's side of the family, and her middle name, Mendenhall, honored Sam's. Their second child, James Nathan, was born in 1893.

J.J. liked Sam, and this, combined with being the son-in-law of the boss, helped his star to rise fast and far. Sam was the first president of the Minneapolis Trust Company, subscribed by 100 investors in 1888, the year Sam and Mary were married, with J.J. contributing $100,000 and Sam $25,000. He became involved with and later was elected vice president of the Minneapolis Athenaeum, founded originally as a private library but which donated its collection of more than 20,000 volumes to the Minneapolis Public Library in 1889. The Minneapolis Trust Company suffered through a financial scandal and 10 years of litigation over the sale of bonds to pay the debts of the failed Northwestern Guarantee Company. Its creditors thought the Trust company should have sold the bonds at a higher price—60 cents on the dollar of debt rather than 10 cents. Although Minneapolis Trust prevailed in the ensuing litigation, the experience soured Sam on Minneapolis and its liberal politics, which were too populist for his Republican views.

Increasingly, his attention turned, or was turned for him by his business responsibilities, to the West. The Montana Central Railroad was built in 1886-87 and linked to the Minneapolis, St. Paul & Manitoba, and then these and other railroads owned by J.J. Hill and his associates were linked as the Great Northern in 1889. By now Sam was the president of 11 companies within his father-in-law's empire, seven of them railroads, and a member of the boards of directors of eight more, four of them railroads including the Great Northern. He also traveled extensively, mostly for business but also for pleasure, particularly to Europe. Although sometimes he traveled with his family, he also made a number of trips alone, including a visit to St. Petersburg in 1899 (he left his family in France); Italy and France in 1900, and then across Siberia by himself in 1901, a journey that was part of a round-the-world trip.

One of his European trips, in 1893, was for the purpose of raising money for the Great Northern, which had halted construction across the western prairies when it ran out of money during the depression that same year. Sam, always a flatterer, had decided that the royal families of Europe had money to spare and might be interested in the novelty, if not also the potential returns, of investing in American businesses. After studying about the various related kings and queens of Europe, Sam decided King Leopold of Belgium would be his best first target. He not only talked his way into an audience with the king, but also sold him a block of Great Northern bonds and, through him, obtained a letter of introduction to England's Queen Victoria, who also became an investor. Victoria recommended Sam meet her granddaughter, Princess Marie of Romania, who then was 17. He did, and later sold another big block of Great Northern bonds to the Romanian royal family.[12]

Over time, Marie would become his friend and confidant and would introduce him to many other members of the European royal families. Sam would visit her frequently on his future European trips, and he felt a particular sympathy for her situation during World War I when the Romanian royal family was forced to flee Bucharest. In 1926 she would tour America, stopping briefly to dedicate Sam's Maryhill estate in the Columbia River Gorge, which he had decided would be a museum. On one of his trips to Europe, he told Marie he would build it and that it would contain a "Romanian Room."

Given his relation to J.J. Hill and his competence as a lawyer and businessman, it would be easy to see Sam as the certain successor to

J.J. Hill, along with J.J.'s sons, in the family business empire, but in 1900 Sam abruptly resigned from his various positions in J.J.'s empire and severed his affiliation with the Great Northern. Something had happened, but it is not clear what. In 1900, Sam was living in Seattle, where he had managed the western affairs of the Great Northern for seven years and where he was president of the Seattle Gas and Electric Company, which had been purchased by investors from Minneapolis and Seattle. Sam's biographer, John Tuhy, suggests that Sam's plan for succession was his alone and not shared by J.J. and the other directors of the Great Northern and its affiliates. Indeed, when J.J. did resign, in 1907, his second son, Louis, succeeded him. At that point, Sam and Louis had been at odds for years over business decisions and also apparently because of their equally strong personalities.

It also is likely that the disintegration of Sam's marriage played a role in his fall from grace within the Hill empire. Certainly J.J. was a devoted father and husband, and perhaps his view of Sam soured as Sam and Mamie, for whom J.J. had great affection, grew increasingly estranged. Sam and Mamie had not been happy for years. After the initial euphoria of their rapid, for the era, high-profile courtship and marriage, family life was mundane and unappealing, and not just to Sam. He busied himself with endless hours of civic works, travel and business. She busied herself with her own civic affairs, and travel, often without Sam. She tried Seattle briefly, when Sam finally convinced her, in 1901, to join him. She arrived in October and was back in St. Paul in the spring of 1902. She returned and gave Seattle another try, but left, with her children, in March 1903. That October, Sam sent a railroad car of her furniture to St. Paul, and she later had it shipped to Washington, D.C., where she had purchased a house.

Sam loved the Pacific Northwest, but Mamie did not. Having spent much time in Washington, D.C., she preferred the cosmopolitan life there to the comparative wilderness of Seattle. They compromised, in a way, and bought an estate in Massachusetts where they would meet with the children, but they never lived together again.

J.J. and Mary Hill were saddened by their daughter's deteriorating marriage, but there was nothing they could do—except be angry with Sam. Tuhy writes, "It seems likely to the author that Sam's later aversion to visiting Minneapolis arose in part from the reaction of some of the Hill clan to the disintegration of the relationship between Sam and Mamie."[13] The marriage "died in all but name," Albro Martin wrote in his biography of J.J. Hill.[14] The effect on their children was pronounced. Mary Mendenhall, prone to depression as a child, slipped further into the mental illness that would kill her in 1941; her brother James lived off the family money and later his inheritance (his mother left him $5.78 million when she died in 1947), in Boston, where he dabbled in Republican politics, collected art, and never distinguished himself in business as Sam had hoped. He also never married, and he seems to have treated his father with indifference.

Meanwhile, Sam thrived in Seattle, melancholy though he was over the state of his marriage and family. He became a tireless promoter of hard-surface roads and highways that would link rural communities to cities, and cities to each other in the Pacific Northwest. He envisioned good roads not only for purposes of commerce, but also for the convenience of long-distance travel and for the pleasure of experiencing natural wonders like the Columbia River Gorge, one of his favorite places.

The Gorge is a 90-mile stretch of the Columbia River through the Cascade Mountains. It is a place of stunning natural beauty. In some areas, the highest peaks fronting on the river rise more than 6,000 feet above its surface.

In 1899, at a time when automobiles were rapidly gaining popularity and becoming more of a necessity of life than an amusement, Sam and a few friends formed the Washington State Good Roads Association. Sam was its president through 1910 and, later, its honorary president for life. He lobbied nationally for good roads beginning in 1900, when he addressed a U.S. Senate committee on the subject. This also was the year of the first National Auto Show.

In 1906, he met Samuel Lancaster, a civil engineer with extensive experience in siting and building roads and railroads. Lancaster was a consulting engineer for the federal Bureau of Public Roads within the Department of Agriculture. The agriculture secretary, James Wilson, sent Lancaster to meet with Sam at a roads conference in Yakima, Washington, to discuss the road situation in the state. The two men quickly became friends, and Sam persuaded Wilson to allow Lancaster to stay six months in Washington to help design roads. After the six months, at Sam's urging, Lancaster resigned his federal post to help design a $7 million system of roads and parks for the 1909 Alaska-Yukon-Pacific Exposition in Seattle. Meanwhile, in 1907 Sam helped persuade the regents of the University of Washington to establish a chair of highway engineering—the first in the nation—with Lancaster as its professor in 1908-09.

Sam, as president of the Washington Good Roads Association, represented the state at the International Road Congress in Paris in October 1908. He took Lancaster and Seattle's city engineer with him, paying their way. The three traveled throughout Europe—it was Sam's 32nd trip to the continent—inspecting roads. Along the Rhine they saw the rock retaining walls that had been built by Charlemagne to support terraces for vineyards, and Sam told Lancaster that one day similar rock walls would support the road he envisioned through the Columbia River Gorge. Later, in an interview with Fred Lockley, Lancaster recalled that Sam told him: "We will build a great highway so that the world can come out and see the beauties of the land out of doors ... and we will realize the magnificence and grandeur of the Columbia River Gorge."

Sam Hill biographer Tuhy called the Columbia River Highway "the Holy Grail" of Sam's campaign for good roads. Sam and Lancaster wanted to build a road that would blend into the remarkable scenery of the Gorge, a road that would become a matter of civic pride. Sam convinced the Multnomah County commissioners and the Oregon Legislature to support the project—he even brought the Legislature to Maryhill in February 1913 to view the experimental roads he had built there. Seattle was beginning to eclipse Portland in population and economic importance, and a new road from Tacoma to Mount Rainier was sure to boost tourism. Portland needed the highway through the Gorge, Sam said.

Rufus Holman, in 1913 a Multnomah County, Oregon, commissioner and later a U.S. senator, called Sam the "playwright and director" of the highway. In an interview after the highway was completed, Holman recalled that he visited the Gorge with Sam in May 1913. There the two men stood on a cliff over the river at sunset and Sam said, "envision for me a wonderful road through that wild canyon . . . a road such as no one had yet seen."

The Columbia River Highway through the Gorge, linking west of Portland to a highway along the river to the coast, was completed in the summer of 1915. By November the road was open to Pendleton, in eastern Oregon, a distance of more than 300 miles inland from the coast. The highway was dedicated in June 1916 with a ceremony at Multnomah Falls.

Lancaster and Sam went on to other projects. Lancaster designed a road along the north rim of the Grand Canyon; Sam built a war memorial in the shape of Stonehenge to honor soldiers from Klickitat County, Washington, who died in World War I. The Stonehenge replica is just off U.S. Highway 97, north of the Columbia River. The Highway 97 bridge at that location is named in honor of Sam. He also built the Peace Arch at Blaine, on the border of Washington and British Columbia. The arch honors a century of peace between the United States and Canada, from the 1814 Treaty of Ghent that established most of the border between the two countries, to 1915.

Maryhill Museum, however, is another story, a lasting tribute to the unique, if skewed, vision of its builder. Maryhill, Washington, is the name of both a small unincorporated community on the shore of the river at the north end of the Sam Hill Memorial Bridge, and also the museum, which sits high in a bluff about three miles to the west. Both are about 100 miles east of Portland, Oregon, and Vancouver, Washington.

Sam planned the community of Maryhill, named in honor of his wife and daughter, as an agricultural paradise "where the rain and sunshine meet," as he liked to say. In 1907, Sam began working to build a new community in the eastern Columbia River Gorge near the ferry-terminal town of Columbus, Washington, which had been settled in the 1860s. Sam later would say he picked the location after consulting maps to determine the ideal location for an agricultural paradise, but it also is likely that he knew about the area because he was familiar with the route of a proposed railroad spur from Spokane to Vancouver, Washington, and Portland, along the north, or Washington, bank of the river. That line, the Spokane, Portland & Seattle, would be completed in 1909. He also had considered, in 1905, building a water power plant at the mouth of the Klickitat River and a straw board factory in the adjacent community of Lyle. The Klickitat River, a Columbia tributary, is about 30 miles to the west, downstream, from Columbus/Maryhill.

Sam also knew that several farms in the area were quite productive, particularly for tree fruits, and that the prosperous apple-growing district around Hood River, Oregon, was about 40 miles downstream. Also, good timber was available a short distance north of Columbus. If the Spokane, Portland & Seattle built a station, and if settlers flocked to Maryhill to farm and build houses in his little city, well, the rest would be history.

The prosperity, however, didn't happen. Hill imagined that the warm and sunny conditions east of the Cascade Mountains and the rainfall west of the mountains somehow would meet in the Maryhill area and provide ideal growing conditions. In fact, the area is in the rain shadow of the mountains and receives only 11 inches of precipitation per year, on average, hardly enough for the acres of fruits and vegetables Sam envisioned. Downstream at Hood River, by comparison, precipitation was nearly double—such is the nature of the rain shadow. Also unlike the productive Hood River valley, the soil at Maryhill was good for crops only near the Columbia; the soil quickly became thin and rocky away from the river, the legacy of repeated catastrophic floods at the end of the last ice age. And there is near-constant wind; summers are hot and dry, winters are cold and harsh.

Nonetheless, the railroad stopped at Columbus/Maryhill, and after Sam succeeded in attracting a few new farmers to the area, he established a ferry crossing. While the farms produced some notably good tree fruits, the production never was large-scale, and by 1914 Sam's grand plans for a community of paved roads, new homes and surrounding productive agricultural fields had failed. He blamed the state of Washington largely, as he believed the lack of a state highway along the north shore of the river was a fatal blow to his community. But in reality, he simply chose a bad location. The ferry service wasn't a great success, either. The service from Maryhill to Biggs, Oregon, began on Feb. 23, 1915, but did not last long. Like Maryhill itself, the ferry service was poorly located. The boat rolled hard in the frequently strong winds and wind-blown waves of the Gorge. It was a side-wheeler, and so with one side partially out of the water on windy crossings, the other side overworked to keep the boat moving. During low water the ferry often hit bottom on a mid-river gravel bar, and during high water the clearance below the Union Pacific Railroad bridge on the Oregon shore was too low for the ferry.

Undisuaded, as was his nature, in spite of the conspiracy of geography, geology, and climate against his grand plans, in 1914 Sam started construction of his castle-like home on a bluff overlooking the river three miles west of the Maryhill community. The site was on the western edge of his 6,000-acre ranch. The building was not completed in his lifetime. Planned as his "ranch house," he never lived there, and his wife, for whom it is at least partly named, never saw it.

Maryhill the ranch house has been called absurdly grand and absurdly located. Sam was proud of it, though, and he commented once that he expected it to be standing a thousand years after he died, and it might be. Like the home he built on East Highland Drive on Capitol Sam in Seattle, Maryhill has thick concrete walls reinforced with steel. No wood was used in its construction. The structure is rectangular, with the long ends facing east and west. Long ramps lead up to the main floor on these ends, stretching the entire structure to some 400 feet. Hill intended the ramps to facilitate guests arriving by car—they could literally drive into one side of the home, drop off passengers, and then exit the other side. The three-story building measures 60 by 93 feet, and is 50 feet tall.

Sam told writer Fred Lockley in 1915 that he chose the site for its scenic beauty and that he planned only "a good, comfortable and substantial farmhouse." Probably he intended it to complement Maryhill, the community on the river far below, and probably he envisioned lavish parties. He did enjoy entertaining people.

Sam did not apply his usual frenetic energy to the construction of Maryhill. He was preoccupied at the time with construction of the Columbia River Highway, and he was experiencing some financial difficulties with his Home Telephone Company in Portland. But in 1919 he sold his holdings to the Bell company, and his finances improved. His plans for Maryhill were changing, as well. That same year he reportedly offered it to the Belgian government as a colonial outpost and a place to honor Belgium's defense against the German invasion of 1914. If the offer actually was made, it was declined. By then he had decided, at the suggestion of his friend Loie Fuller, an American dancer and artist of international fame, to make Maryhill a museum rather than a home.

The museum was incorporated in 1923. Queen Marie of Romania, who toured the United States in 1926 largely at Sam's insistence, dedicated the unfinished hulk of a building in November of that year in a lavish ceremony. But the hulk was not destined to remain empty and wind-blown. Some of Sam's wealthy and influential friends, including Loie Fuller and Alma Spreckels, she of the Hawaiian sugar fortune, stepped up. Alma Spreckels donated some of her collection and also helped secure other artworks for the museum, including sculptures by Auguste Rodin, a friend of both women. The museum opened to the public on May 13, 1940, which would have been Sam's 83rd birthday.

The Maryhill experiment, the Columbia River Highway, and Sam's growing business interests in Portland demonstrate an important point about this time in his life: increasingly he was souring on Seattle. In fact, he had been turning his attention increasingly to southern Washington and to Oregon ever since 1907, when he began working on Maryhill, the community and the ranch. Despite his conservative leanings, the more progressive Oregon, in his view at least, attracted his attention. The Columbia River Gorge, Maryhill notwithstanding, would be the site of his next big schemes and accomplishments.

Part of his disillusionment with Washington had to do with his passion, road-building. In 1911, Sam thought he had convinced Governor Marion Hay to allow state prison convicts to continue building roads in Klickitat County, where Sam had convinced farmers that the roads would provide quick, efficient access to the ferry dock at Lyle and reduce the cost of transporting grain to market. Construction had been halted because the Klickitat County commissioners balked at the expense. At the last minute, with construction about to restart, Hay backpedaled and sent the convicts back to prison. Sam was infuriated, and he campaigned hard for his friend Ernest Lister, Hay's opponent, when the governor ran for re-election in 1912. Lister won. Even for Lister, though, the cost of the north bank road was too high despite the use of convict labor. Washington, for Sam, was increasingly unprogressive.

Sam also found reason to complain about his treatment in Seattle, where his relations with civic leaders had become increasingly frosty. In 1920, when the City Council voted to build a reservoir in Volunteer Park, over his objections, he wrote to the Council to complain that its existence uphill from his home would endanger property all the way down the hill to Lake Union. He went on to list his many—and to his mind underappreciated—good works on behalf of Seattle, such as promoting street paving, endowing chairs at the University of Washington in road engineering and Russian language, promoting Seattle as a port for trade with western Pacific nations, and so on. It was a sort of Dear-John letter, a breakup and parting of two friends who simply were going in opposite directions, and for Sam that direction was south to Portland. After the election of 1912, Sam regularly split his time between Seattle and Portland, leaving the great house on Capitol Hill empty for weeks, and sometimes months.

All of the myriad facets of Sam's complicated life—his failed marriage, his disappointing children, his love of the Columbia River Gorge, his promotion of good roads, his wealth, and his interest in international travel—were evident in the events that unfolded late in his life, in the 1920s. His Peace Arch at Blaine was dedicated in 1921. He made a trip around the world in 1922 and was awarded "The Third Class Order of the Sacred Treasure" in Japan, where he had visited several times previously to promote business relations with American companies and, of course, construction of good roads. He became the president of a coal mine in Alabama in 1923. He hosted Queen Marie on her U.S. tour in 1926, and he continued to lobby for the construction of the elusive north bank road along the Columbia River.

His personal life, though, was a shambles. Mamie would not agree to a divorce because of her Catholic faith. She continued to live in Washington, D.C., with the children. There were occasional visits, Sam sometimes traveling east to the capital or to their estate in Massachusetts, and his children sometimes coming west.[15]

Sam loved his children, but ultimately they disappointed him. Mary had a mental illness and James was aloof, disinterested in Sam's businesses, and unambitious. Most importantly to Sam, his children were not having families of their own, and so there were no heirs apparent. Tuhy suggests, "Surely by design and not through accident, [Sam] sired three children by other women as a defiant answer to a fate bent on thwarting his dreams."[16]

Sam established a trust fund for each of those children. Nothing today is known of one of the women, not even her name. Evidently she was British, however, as her son was born in England and adopted by a family named Palmer. David Palmer eventually settled in British Columbia, where he operated a heavy equipment business. The second of Sam's mistresses was Annie Laurie Whelan, whose father was a friend of J.J. and Mary Hill in St. Paul. Beginning in 1902, Annie worked for Sam as his secretary at the Seattle Gas Company, and then later for his land company at Maryhill and his Home Telephone Company in Portland. She left the telephone company when she became pregnant. Her daughter, Elisabeth, was born in October 1914 in New York. Annie had income from the sale of Home Telephone Company bonds and also was the beneficiary of Sam's six life insurance policies. After Sam's death, the proceeds of the insurance policies were paid to Annie, and when the bonds matured in 1936, the income was re-invested for the benefit of Elisabeth. She graduated from Stanford that same year with a degree in architecture, married in 1940, and eventually had three children. Annie died in California in 1942. Elisabeth Wade died in 2008. Her trust reverted to Maryhill Museum, a requirement Sam put in each of the trusts—upon the death of the child, the remaining amount of the trust would be paid to the museum. Interestingly, in its March 2009 newsletter, the museum listed among its recent donations one from Sam Hill of "$1,000,000 and above." The same newsletter reported on Elisabeth's death, identifying her as Sam's daughter. David Palmer, meanwhile, apparently still was living as his trust had not reverted to the museum.

The third mistress was Mona Bell, and she could not have been more different in terms of her personality and background from the shy, quiet Annie Whelan or the imperious Mamie Hill.

"Mona Bell was kind of stiff with a hug," Mona's daughter-in-law, Virginia Hill, said in a 2007 interview. "She didn't really know how to be a mother. She was a woman alone."

CHAPTER 3

A Woman Alone

ROM THE TIME MONA BELL LEFT HOME, PROBABLY IN 1908 WHEN SHE WAS 18, SHE WAS SOMETHING OF A GYPSY, TRAVELING THE COUNTRY FROM NEW YORK CITY WHERE SHE WORKED FOR THE STREET-CAR advertising firm, to San Francisco, where she worked as a newspaper reporter. She seemed to live life as a dare, trying this career or that, never staying long in one place. There is almost no surviving record of her travels and stops, other than the recollections of her son and some of her other relatives and, curiously, post cards that were saved by her sister, Frances, and passed to her daughter, Mona's niece Bonnie Evans. The 20 cards include nine addressed to Mona in East Grand Forks—with the exception of one addressed to her at the University of North Dakota. The rest were sent by Mona to her sister or mother from various stops on Mona's itinerate travels, some more permanent than others.

The post cards sent to Mona when she still lived at home are from friends, apparently, and not relatives, as the names do not correspond to any in Mona's immediate family. They are chatty and brief. One, dated September 7, 1908, is signed "bob" and postmarked in San Francisco, which he described as "a mostly beautiful place." He adds, "Hope you are having a fine time." Another, dated Feb. 3, 1909, is signed, "Ted," whose one-sentence greeting was "Why don't you write?" The postmark is "World's Fair Seattle 1909," which would have been the Alaska-Pacific Yukon Exposition, which Sam Hill helped organize. Three other post cards are addressed to her at East Grand Forks in 1909, one in April, one in July, and one in early September. But later that month, September 1909, Mona wrote to her mother, Esther, from Spokane, Washington, where she evidently took a job as a teacher. She writes: "Arrived and am staying with Mrs. Shropshire. Will probably start teaching the last of the week. She is spoiling me altogether. The trip out here was a beautiful one. Will write you later and tell you all." The card is signed, "Edith."

While there is no record today to verify it, Mona probably taught for the International Correspondence Schools of Scranton, PA (ICS), whose local agent was Harry P. Shropshire. The school, founded in 1895 and reorganized in 1905 following bankruptcy, provided distance-learning classes in mining industry skills and trades; Spokane was the center of the Inland Northwest mining industry. At the time, the ICS did not have branch campuses, with the exception of one in London and another in Canada. The Spokane ICS office probably was a sales office, where the local agents coordinated enrollment and possibly developed coursework and met with students.[17]

The school's correspondence courses ranged widely—building construction, electricity, masonry, steel casting. Based on her coursework at the University of North Dakota, Mona could have taught writing or English, or helped to draft course materials that were mailed to students. The Spokane campus or facility was located on Main Street in the downtown area, and Mona's residence—and also the residence of the Shropshires—was seven blocks east in the Empire Hotel, according to the 1909 Spokane City Directory. Mona's listing in the directory does not indicate her occupation.

It appears she stayed in Spokane for one year or less; she is not listed in the 1908 or 1910 directories. She received two post cards in Spokane in August 1910, both addressed to her in care of general delivery, Spokane. One is postmarked Pueblo, Colorado, on the 14th and the other is postmarked Denver on the 16th. The inscription on the first reads only "Pueblo, CO, Aug. 12, 1910," and the inscription on the second is "Colorado Springs, CO, Aug. 14, 1910." Both are signed, "Bert."

The post card evidence of Mona's time in Spokane poses an interesting challenge to the story that Mona met Sam Hill in Grand Forks in August 1910 when Buffalo Bill's Wild West performed there. Clearly she was teaching in Spokane and not performing at the time. In fact, if Mona met Sam in Grand Forks in 1910, it would have been later in the year—if they met there at all.

The remaining post cards in the chronology demonstrate Mona's country-crossing lifestyle. In April 1911 she wrote to her mother from Los Angeles, and later that year, in October, sent two cards from Mount

Tamalpais, California, north of San Francisco, one to her mother and the other to her sister, Frances. In both of these, she comments on the lovely scenery. She seems to have been on vacation.

Now the chronology skips two years, to 1913, when Mona wrote to Frances from Corpus Christi, Texas, where she evidently was living. "When are you coming down to visit big sis and see all the pretty places?" she wrote. She signed that card, as she had all of the others, with her first name, Edith. In September, she wrote to Frances from Portland, Oregon, urging her to "hurry and write, don't be so stingy." If she was living in Portland at the time, there is no record of it in Portland's city directory for that year. The post card was one sold by the Southern Pacific Railroad, a pretty scene of a Tudor-style home in Portland surrounded by flowering rhododendrons.

Now the post card chronology skips two more years, to 1915, when Mona wrote to her sister twice in March from the Panama Pacific International Exposition in San Francisco. The first, dated March 6, has the Exposition's postmark and an illustration of the Palace of Liberal Arts. "Dear Little Sis: A letter from you would seem awfully good. Have my eyes open for souvenirs," she wrote. The second, dated on the 9th, is postmarked El Paso, Texas. Perhaps she was traveling home from the fair. The inscription shows her interest in foreign art: "Dear Little sis: sent you a little package by express. Sent you a Japanese cabinet and some Turkish candy and pastry from the Turkish village at the fair. Also a few souvenirs they give away at the different cafes. Blow up the balloon." Then above the "Dear Little sis" is: "Write your sister soon Edith"

A post card later that year, in December, also to Frances, is postmarked St. Louis. "Wished for you in Mpls to share a couple good dinners," she wrote. "Am in the sunny south and is very warm ... will arrive St. Louis in couple of hours. Edith." Was she living in Minneapolis at the time? Or was she still in Texas, traveling by train between the sunny south and the cold north? Mexico was one of Mona's favorite vacation places; perhaps she had been there.

The last post card in the chronology is dated the following year, on July 28, again to Frances in East Grand Forks, postmarked "Hotel Fontenelle, Omaha, Nebraska." "Absolutely shall disown you as my sister if you don't write me oftener little lady," she wrote. She signed the card "Edith Elder," likely a reference to her big-sister position rather than a new last name. She liked to call Frances her "little sis."

There the chronology of Mona's life from the time she was 19 years old until she was 26 ends. Unfortunately, as with so many other aspects of Mona's life, records simply do not exist today to verify her peripatetic career, but her son remembers stories she told him.

"Probably she was the first female crime reporter in the country," Sam, recalled. "At that time she was working for a San Francisco paper. Abe Ruef, an alderman, had been arrested for graft. He was in jail and no one could interview him. My mother got in there, God knows how. She was working on the society page, and she hated it. She got the interview, wrote a story, and offered it to the editor on the condition that she would be made a crime reporter. She was."

Ruef was a brilliant lawyer who could speak eight languages and who became a major crime boss in San Francisco in the late 1890s through his support of organized labor. The Union Labor Party, which he started in 1901, was his primary vehicle, and through the labor organization he funneled bribes to many of San Francisco's elected officials. By 1906, he controlled the city's Board of Supervisors and the Chief of Police, in addition to a couple of judges. But then his fiefdom collapsed when his choice for District Attorney, William Langton, decided not to cooperate and instead exposed the corruption, beginning with the city's unregulated gambling halls and brothels. The *San Francisco Bulletin* and its managing editor, Fremont Older, supported Langton, and Older soon convinced millionaire sugar importer Rudolph Spreckels to finance a federal investigation. This was interrupted by the 1906 earthquake, but when the investigation resumed in 1907 it led to indictments of a number of people, including the mayor and members of the Board of Supervisors. Ruef ended up in San Quentin, where he served five years of a 14-year sentence for bribery, from March 1911 through August 1915. Ironically, he and Older had become friends after Older became convinced that Ruef's sentence was too severe and he helped Ruef plan his appeals, which nonetheless were unsuccessful.

If the story is true, the post card evidence suggests she might have left her teaching job in Spokane for San Francisco in late 1910. The post cards show she was in California in 1911, and two—those from Mount Tamalpais—show she was there in October of that year. They don't indicate, however, whether she was living in the Bay Area at the time or just passing through on one of her trips.

If Mona were working as a reporter in San Francisco, the paper she probably worked for was the *Bulletin*, as its editor at the time was John Bruce. "My mother was a good friend of John Bruce, who eventually became city editor of the [San Francisco] Chronicle, and she used to speak of knowing and admiring Fremont Older," Hill said.

Mona worked as a reporter for many years and always spoke with pride of her journalism career, which included stints in Omaha, Minneapolis, Kansas City, and Portland, in addition to San Francisco. Hill said Mona was a reporter at *The Oregonian* in Portland, but no record of her employment remains today. That doesn't mean she did not write for the paper; most likely, she was a correspondent paid by the story or the column inch, and records of those contract reporters were not retained.

It isn't clear precisely when Mona moved to Portland, but by 1914 Sam was there, or at least he was such a frequent visitor, now splitting his time between Seattle and Portland, that he was listed in the Portland City Directory for the years 1914 and 1915. The 1914 City Directory lists his occupation as president of the Home Telephone Company of Portland and his address as the Arlington Club, which was on Salmon Street between Park and West Park (Ninth Avenue today). The following year his address is on South Broadway in downtown Portland. He is not listed again in a Portland city directory.

Sam took over the Home Telephone Company in 1909. Beginning in 1910, the year he met Mona, Sam brought his daughter, Mary Mendenhall Hill, to live with him in Seattle and Portland in periodic, extended visits. In 1916 she was hospitalized at St. Vincent's Hospital in Portland, where she stayed for three months for treatment of a mental illness. By the description of her symptoms, it probably was schizophrenia. In December 1914, while Sam was living in Portland, his second mistress, Annie Whelan, gave birth to his daughter in New York City. It is not clear today whether Mona knew about Annie, or if so, ever met her. It seems clear, though, that Mona kept in touch with Sam over the years. One of her nieces recalled her mother telling stories about Mona's liaisons with Sam when he traveled.

Little else is known about Mona's life before she gave birth to her and Sam's son in Portland in 1928. There are family stories, however, which have gained credence through repetition if not actual proof. For example, her son said Mona covered herself with grease and swam across the Strait of Juan de Fuca between Washington state and Vancouver Island a year or two before Gertrude Ederle famously swam across the English Channel. For the record, at its narrowest point, the Strait of Dover, the English Channel, is 21 miles across; the Strait of Juan de Fuca is between 10 and 18 miles across, and the water there is colder and rougher.

While Mona's swim, if it happened, didn't attract press attention, her rodeo career did, although briefly. The Circus World Museum Library in Baraboo, Wisconsin, has in its collection a single story about Mona. The article ran in Billboard Magazine on May 9, 1931, and described her as a cowgirl radio artist, singing old-time and cowboy songs as part of a western concert. In the same show, she also worked with ponies and in a double-bull act.[18] This was with the Schell Bros. Circus, based in Manteca, California. Circus acts were different than those in a wild west show—no bronc-riding or trick shooting, but the Schell Bros. show had plenty of animals, including an elephant. According to the *Billboard* article, which described a performance in Lebanon, Oregon, on April 27, 1931, the show had been on the road for five weeks and had traveled 1,725 miles so far. The article doesn't say how many shows the circus would put on that year, but it was so popular in Lebanon that straw had to be spread beyond the usual seating area to accommodate all the customers.

No doubt the circus drew extra patrons because the owner-manager George Engesser had signed the famous Jack Hoxie, a bonafide cowboy who went from ranch hand and Army scout in Oklahoma and Idaho to Hollywood movie star, appearing in more than 40 silent films as a cowboy and gunslinger. By 1931 his star was fading, but he still was a big draw. The *Billboard* article comments: "Jack Hoxie, Western film star, and his entire Hollywood company have proved a good moneymaker for the show." In detailing the performance, which included 24 separate "displays," the article describes Mona's role: "Band Leader C.B. Brooks and his musicians have a finely selected program, ranging from popular to classical pieces interspersed with airs and songs by the prima dona, Mona Bell." She worked high school ponies in Display 17, which followed a performance by a clown band, and took part in Display 18, a two-ring, double-bull act. In all, the show included 65 trucks to carry all the equipment, numerous cages for the animals, 20 mounted riders, and three bands.

Mona's stints in advertising and journalism, her performances with the circus, the frigid swim across the Strait, her marksmanship—she prided herself on her accuracy with pistols and rifles—and her interest in basketball make a point about Mona's personality that would be evident to others, family and friends, all her life. She wanted to prove that she could do anything a man could do.

"She really resented being told she couldn't do things because she was a woman," her son, Sam, said.

While she appears to have wandered across the country both as tourist and as itinerant journalist and teacher through the teens and early 1920s, she settled in Portland, Oregon, in 1928. That year Mona is listed in the Portland City Directory. She was 38 years old and pregnant with Sam's child. Mona is listed under her maiden name—Edith M. Bell—at 725 Irving St., Apt. 11.

The Irving address was about two miles north of the Multnomah County Hospital, where Sam B. Hill was born on August 11, 1928. Mona's sister, Frances Thoms, was with her, having traveled from her home in East Grand Forks, Minnesota, for the birth. Sam Hill, the proud father, sent a congratulatory telegram from Blaine, Washington, at 1:40 p.m. the day of the birth, a Saturday, addressed to Frances. The telegram read: "Delighted Will arrive Monday morning." Evidently, Frances or Mona had sent him a telegram announcing the birth.

Sam's telegram was addressed to Frances Thoms at the San Carlos Apartments. According to the 1928 Portland City Directory, the address of the apartments was 195 S.W. Vista Ave. Two months later, in October, Mona registered to vote in Multnomah County, listing her residence as 195 S.W. Vista Ave. and her last name as Hill (the San Carlos Apartments still exist, but the street number has changed to 835 S.W. Vista). On the registration card she lists her husband's name as Edgar. The following year, 1929, the city directory lists Mona's address as 918 Capitol Avenue and her last name as Hill, but she is not listed as the wife of Edgar Hill and there is no separate listing for him. Neither Mona nor Edgar appear in subsequent Portland directories, but Mona was listed in a 1935 directory of residents of rural Multnomah County under the name Hill, Mona B. Her address is "P.O. Bonneville," and she is described: "owns 34 1/2 acres; assd. $4,100." Again, there is no mention of Edgar Hill.

Edgar Hill was Sam's cousin. After Mona became pregnant, Sam arranged for his cousin to marry her. The date of the marriage is not known today, but probably it was early in the year. Edgar was an executive in at least two of Sam's businesses, the United States Trust Company and Samuel Hill, Inc.

Born in 1861, and thus four years younger than Sam, Edgar had been married before, in July 1893 in Indiana. The 1900 Census of Indiana, however, lists him as divorced. He was living in Carthage, Indiana, at the time, where he was a banker and also a principal in the U.S. Board and Paper Company. He moved to Seattle in 1906 at Sam's invitation. That year he sold his interest in the paper company and resigned as an officer. He wrote to Sam that he was ready to move West and invest $25,000 wherever Sam thought best.

Now, 22 years later and one of Sam's confidants, Edgar agreed to be married to Sam's mistress. Sam's son James recalled in a 1946 letter to Sam's cousin David Hill that the marriage took place in Portland. However, no record of the marriage of Edgar and Mona could be located in state or county vital records archives in Oregon or Washington. Either the records don't exist or there never were records in the first place. That might be the case because Virginia Hill says Mona told her Sam himself performed the marriage ceremony and that it was private.

"Sam was a Quaker, and as a practicing Quaker he could preside at a wedding," Virginia Hill said. "The only thing we ever were told was that either Sam or Mona wanted the child to have the Hill name. Knowing her, she would not have wanted to show that she was having a child out of wedlock; it would have been horrible in those days. So that might have been some pressure, or maybe Sam was kind enough to offer and say, you know, I'll get my cousin to do this."[19]

Quakers traditionally eschewed oath-taking, and this prohibition included filing government records of marriages. When a couple chose to marry within the Quaker church, they were taken under the care of the Friends meeting where they attended Sunday services. Over a period of time, sometimes months, members of the meeting would advise the couple about marriage and its responsibilities. When the couple decided the time was right, they would declare to the congregation their intention to marry and all present would sign a certificate of marriage. Quaker marriages were recognized as legal, even though there was no formal government document. Every meeting had leaders, and these would officiate at Sunday services including those where couples were married.

Lorraine Watson, pastor of the North Seattle Friends Church, the successor congregation to one Sam helped financially in 1907,[20] said it would be outside normal practice for Sam to have married Mona and Edgar.

"To my knowledge, Sam Hill was not an active participant in the life of the church other than the generous gift and assistance with building the original church building," she said. "He is not listed in our membership records. It is possible that Sam Hill could have followed his understanding of Quaker marriage practice and officiated at such a wedding, but that would be unusual for a Quaker as it would have been outside the Quaker community. In general, Quakers took very seriously the commitment to the meeting and would not act outside the sense of that meeting."

Despite his generosity to the Seattle Monthly Meeting, it does not appear Sam was a regular attendee of any church. He hoped to attract Quaker farmers to his land around Maryhill, and in anticipation he initiated a Friends meeting at the Maryhill community. The Maryhill meeting convened exactly one service, on Aug. 29, 1909. The Quaker farmers didn't flock to the place where Sam envisioned the rain and the sunshine meeting, and so his plans for a Quaker meeting evaporated. Thus it is unlikely Edgar and Mona were under the care of any Quaker community when they were married, other than the community of Sam, so to speak.

"As far as I know, there was just the two of them and Sam Hill, and that was it. He was the minister," Virginia Hill said.

Imagine the scene, if it actually happened: A married man presiding over the nominal wedding of his mistress, pregnant with his child, to his cousin. It gives new meaning to the term "family ties."

However bizarre the circumstances of Mona's wedding, the marriage did serve to tie Mona to Edgar Hill, legally or not. Regardless of whether Sam performed the ceremony, he did establish a $60,000 trust fund for the baby's benefit and built Mona a hilltop mansion at his favorite place, and hers, in the Columbia River Gorge.

CHAPTER 4

The Mansion Atop Bonneville Rock

*H*IRAM A. LEAVENS WAS BORN IN NEW YORK IN 1824 OR 1825. HE WAS TRAINED AS A DOCTOR AND DRUGGIST AND MARRIED IN 1849 IN ILLINOIS. HE AND HIS WIFE, PLUMA, CAME WEST ON THE OREGON Trail in 1852 and settled near Cascade Locks, Oregon.

In 1866 he filed a Donation Land Claim for 318 acres along the south shore of the Columbia River west of Cascade Locks, near the lower end of the Cascades Rapids.[21] His land was across the Columbia River from Beacon Rock, then called Castle Rock. Hi, as he was called, was the first doctor and druggist in Cascade Locks and also conducted surveys for road construction in the area, a small community about 45 miles east of Portland.

In October 1901, David O. Leavens, a son of Hiram and Pluma, patented 80 acres adjacent to his parents' land to the east.[22] On Jan. 5, 1915, David Leavens sold 40 acres of this parcel to Henry L. Davis of Maryhill, Washington. Davis was a first cousin of Sam Hill, one of three cousins Sam brought west to join his business ventures.[23] Excluded from the sale to Davis were two rights of way reserved by David Leavens, one apparently for his personal use and the other granted to Multnomah County for construction of the Columbia River Highway.

On Nov. 28, 1917, Davis sold two small parcels on the north side of the Columbia River Highway at the western edge of the larger parcel, one to a woman named Hazel Alice Potter and the other to Richard W. Montague, a Portland attorney, and his wife, Ellen. Hazel Potter was the wife of J.C. Potter, one of Sam's partners in the Home Telephone Company of Portland. Richard Montague represented Sam in certain investment dealings.

On the same day, Davis sold the remaining approximately 34 1/2 acres, minus the rights of way, to Sam Hill's investment company, the United States Trust Company of Seattle.

It was a beautiful piece of property. Dense with fir and pine, the land sloped gently from south to north toward the river, ending in a large area of flat land along the water. There was a singular exception to this otherwise level to gently sloping parcel: a prominent hill that occupied most of the front, northeastern third of the property. The heavily timbered promontory rose to about 200 feet above the river and was mostly flat on top—and also easily accessible from the long east side. On the other three sides, the hill, known locally as Bonneville Rock, was steep and in some places its solid basalt core was exposed in great, columnar protrusions. In all, the property was dramatic and ideally situated for stunning views from atop the rock and for river access and potential residential and commercial development below.

The teens and '20s were busy years for Sam. He completed the Columbia River Highway and continued to oversee his many business ventures, increasingly turning his attention—and frustration—to the struggling Home Telephone Company in Portland, which faced ruthless competition from Pacific Telephone and Telegraph. He also continued to travel extensively. In 1916, for example, he traveled to Russia to help straighten out the unworkable road and rail transportation network around Vladivostok.

When Sam finally sold the Home Telephone Company—or rather when it passed into receivership and was sold on the steps of the Multnomah County courthouse in February 1919—Sam and other bondholders realized about 70 cents on the dollar of their investments; the stockholders got nothing. Competition with the Bell System and Sam's overcapitalization of the company—reported to be more than twice the value of the stock—contributed to the local telephone company's demise. Sam clung to hope that he could salvage the independent company in the face of competition from the behemoth Pacific Telephone, but it was not to be. Always stubborn, Sam didn't let go until the end. If he had given up earlier, he might have saved some of his investors from big losses. Hill biographer John Tuhy faults Sam's "combination of stubbornness and ego" for "another casualty."[26]

But the influx of cash gave Sam a little extra cushion to spend on several of his new projects, including the Stonehenge Memorial (1918), the Peace Arch at Blaine on the Washington/British Columbia border

(1920), a restaurant and golf course at Semiahmoo, in northwestern Washington near Blaine, and a coal mine in Alabama. The Peace Arch was dedicated in 1921, Sam travelled around the world in 1922 with his friend Marshall Joseph Joffre of France and a large party, continued work on the Maryhill Museum, and escorted Queen Marie on her American tour in 1926. There is an unconfirmed—and unconfirmable— report that Mona was with Sam when Marie dedicated the museum and was asked to remain in the crowd of onlookers or in Sam's car to avoid being seen with him in public.

On Oct. 1, 1928, the United States Trust Company deeded the Bonneville property to Sam's real estate holding company, Samuel Hill, Incorporated[27], and one day later, on Oct. 2, 1928, Samuel Hill, Incorporated, sold the property to Mona Bell—officially, the deed says "E. Bell Hill," for $1[28]. Baby Sam was two months old.

Thus, Mona became the owner of the hilltop and the flat and buildable land to the north and south along the Columbia. The area, while unincorporated, nonetheless was a small community at the time. Since the completion of the Columbia River Highway, the area had been a popular spot with picnickers, and the Oregon Railroad and Navigation Company operated an all-you-can-eat dining hall at the Bonneville[29] depot for its passengers.

While Mona officially became the owner of her property in October, the mansion may have been completed earlier in the year. "She was her own general contractor," her son, Sam B. Hill, said in a 1985 interview.

No official record of the construction, such as a building permit, survives. But there is anecdotal evidence that the mansion, which stood at what was then the western edge of Bonneville Rock, was built in 1928. In a 1984 letter to Nancy Russell of Portland, who then directed the Friends of the Columbia River Gorge, Francis W. "Tex" Sloat of Ridgefield, Washington, wrote that he visited Mona at her mansion in the summer or fall of 1928 when he was working for the Forest Service at the Herman Ranger Station. Part of his job was to patrol the Gorge between Warrendale and Hood River during the fire season. Sloat contacted Mona about a permit she requested for a slash fire on her property. "The house was built when I was there . . . I remember the long winding driveway with many shrubs and flowers," he wrote. In an interview in 1985, Sloat recalled spirea, myrtle, and pink locust bushes lining the driveway to the top of the hill. Mona was very friendly, he said, adding, "she wore coveralls and was working in the yard."

On June 6, 1928, Mona was granted a water permit by Multnomah County for a diversion of 0.03 cubic feet per second from an unnamed creek that was a tributary of the Columbia River. According to the permit, the purpose of the diversion was: "Domestic, including irrigation of lawn and garden."[30]

A landscape irrigation plan prepared by Paul Doty and dated June 1928 shows a pipeline more than 1,000 feet long beginning at a cistern adjacent to the unnamed creek, then running north down the hill and under the Columbia River Highway, and finally up to the hilltop. Four branches from the main line carried water to rotating sprinklers and a fish pond that was in front of the house. In all, the irrigated area was about an acre.

While it is clear who designed the irrigation system, it is not clear today who designed the house. Paul E. Doty was president of Doty and Doerner, a Portland landscaping firm. While possibly related, Paul Doty and Harold W. Doty should not be confused. Harold Doty, an architect, designed some of Portland's most notable residences in the 1920s and 1930s while affiliated with another distinguished Portland architect, Wade Hampton Pipes. Doty and Pipes were known for their exquisite arts and crafts designs, featuring steep roofs and prominent gables. Mona's house had gables, but the roof pitch, gable and turret size in proportion to the rest of the house, and many other disparate design elements made it a kind of architectural hash, according to reviews by prominent, modern-day architectural historians in Portland.

After reviewing photos of the house, one of these experts, Henry C. Kunowski of Historical Research Associates, Inc., wrote:

"This one and one-half story residence is a basic "L-Shaped Plan" creating a 1 1/2 story front Gable end and a 1-story Gable side elevation at the north elevation entry. A two-story Norman Turret is located at the apex of the "L" and serves as the main entrance portal. A masonry chimney is located between the Entry Turret and the 1 1/2 story Gable end. The second story gable end

elevation contains a tri-art double-hung wood window system, and the first story level contains a hipped-roof oriel bay with a large fixed multi-pane steel sash window on the front elevation and half-timber framing on the oriel bay. The remainder of the elevation is a heavy stucco finish of the "California" style texture. The upper level of the turret is fully stuccoed with the first story level finished in half-timber and slightly recessed under the upper floor level creating an overhang. The single story level of the residence contains half-timbers and a series of double-hung windows. The [side facing the Gorge] is dominated by a near full-width gable end wall dormer suggesting a vaulted ceiling on the interior with an array of windows. A single story half-timber garage is located off the one-story "L" at the gable end to the [north].

"Overall, the proportions of the residence and a number of the details are awkward in their design execution. The second level of the turret is large for the composition of the gable-end, and its untrimmed recessed windows seem small given the mass of the Turret. Further, the smaller western side first level with its half-timbering appears overwhelmed by the top heavy nature of the turret. The gable end oriel bay is proportional to the elevation, but the half-timbering with the large multi-pane window appears too small for the bay proportion."

Kunowski summed up his appraisal this way: "From the description noted above and the awkward proportions and details of the residence, it does not appear that the house was designed by the hand of a notable architect or designer."[31]

Given that Mona was the general contractor, according to her son, it is likely she had a heavy hand in the design, hiring an architect—any architect would do—and dictating the particulars. Despite its uneven pedigree, it was a big house even by modern-day standards—either 20 or 22 rooms, both numbers have been reported—on one-and-a-half stories. The turret on the front of the house was matched, in a sense, at the back of the house by a half-circular breakfast room off the kitchen on the main floor and, above, a covered balcony off the master bedroom. The view from either direction would have been stunning, as the structure was situated at about a 30-degree angle to the river, affording commanding views to the east, north, and particularly west.

In June 1928, when the water permit was issued, Mona was seven months pregnant and must have known that the house and the land would be hers, even though the transfer would not be made officially until October. When the baby was born in August, Mona named him after his father, at least his first and last names. It isn't clear whether Sam helped choose the name, but the baby's middle name, Bettle, was a revered family name among Sam's Quaker ancestors, Virginia Hill, Mona's daughter in law, said. By 1929, the house was finished and Mona and young Sam were living there alone, except for a cook and gardener, and those two actually lived elsewhere.

For a couple of years, at least, life was peaceful, even idyllic and occasionally controversial as the result of Mona's reputation in the Bonneville community. She busied herself in her extensive garden, may have been a correspondent for *The Oregonian*, although no clippings or records of that work survive, and served as a Multnomah County reserve deputy sheriff.

Mona made her mansion a showplace. Imagine the pristine view of the stately river from her hilltop, stretching away for miles to the East toward misty sunrises and to the west toward sunsets that could paint the sky with a palette of reds and purples and highlight the dramatic landscape, Beacon Rock jutting out of the water before a backdrop of steep mountains towering several thousand feet. Just 40 miles away to the west was bustling Portland, with its shopping and entertainment, the transportation and cultural hub of the region, but on her hilltop Mona could find a spiritual and emotional peace amid the nature she loved so much. She created a lovely estate, a place where she worked tirelessly outdoors to create an unusual and inviting mix of plants and water, mixing the exotic and ornamental among the native plants lining the drive up the hill to her front door, a drive that culminated in a circle around the fish pond.

She enjoyed the unusual, and her home became a sort of museum for objects she acquired on her travels. On a trip to Europe she had visited a monastery in France, where she admired a dining table and matching hutch. She made a sketch and, upon returning to the United States, commissioned reproductions from a furniture company in Michigan. The table and hutch were in her Bonneville mansion, which she also furnished with comfortable furniture and expensive fixtures, including lamps by the Rembrandt company.

Outdoors she had many exotic plants and bushes on the grounds. These included imported tree peonies and a special hybrid of rhododendron that came from India, along with flowering shrubbery that Sam brought from Japan.

"She loved the house, but she loved the landscaping even more," Virginia Hill, said. "Whenever she talked about the house, she talked about the landscaping. That was her love, really her love. It was incredible to see her with her plants."

Mona entertained frequently, occasionally hosting Sam and his important friends. Her guests included the wealthy Adolph and Alma Spreckels of San Francisco, who inherited the family sugar plantations in Hawaii and who later purchased some of the art for the Maryhill Museum including sculptures by Auguste Rodin. Alma Spreckels took one, and probably two, of the few remaining photographs of Mona's mansion. On the back of one of the three-by-five-inch black-and-white photos is an inscription in Alma's trademark large handwriting in purple ink: "Mona Bell's house at Bonneville damn." The original is at the Maryhill Museum. Another photo that is the same size and could have been taken at the same time, perhaps also by Alma, shows the south side of the house. There is a picnic table in the foreground with what looks like a magazine and writing tablet on top, and nearby a woman in a white dress standing partially behind a fir tree. There is no inscription or other identifying information on the photo, which an archivist found at Bonneville Dam among a collection of construction photos from the 1930s. The photo is now in the National Archives in Seattle.

Mona didn't talk publicly about her relationship with Sam Hill, at least not later in her life and probably not at the time she lived on the hilltop, either. Publicly, she was—or had been—married to Sam's cousin, Edgar, and they may have been divorced or he might have died.[32] At any rate, she was alone, but the Hill name gave her a kind of shirt-tail connection to

Sam, and if people suspected he was the father of her child, that was just speculation and rumor.

It was no secret, however, that Sam built the mansion for Mona. For example, in the records of the Real Estate Office of the Portland District of the U.S. Army Corps of Engineers are copies of two mechanic's liens, one dated Nov. 6, 1930, for $130 and the other dated Jan. 17, 1931 for $936.84.[33] The latter was filed by Hansen and Liejequist, Inc., a Portland business, for material used in the construction of the house, and the former was filed by a man named Frank Bird who sought compensation for "material and labor used in the construction, alteration, and repair" of the house. The lien names "Monobelle Hill and Saml Hill" as defendants. Bonneville was a small place before the hoards of construction workers began to arrive, and it is possible, even likely, that a dispute over labor and construction of such a magnificent structure would have been known among the local residents, and the names of Sam and Mona linked in connection with the house and each other.

Mona had developed a reputation in the Bonneville community for being aloof, at times, but she also was seen regularly with her son. Harold Bailey, a Bonneville resident from 1922 to 1942, didn't know Mona personally but knew about her. He heard stories about Mona from his mother, who was the telegraph operator at the Bonneville railroad depot. She was a friend of Mona's houseboy.

"I was in her [Mona's] place just once before she left," Bailey said in a 1985 interview. "She leased several rooms in her house to the government surveyors for the Bonneville project. She was up there on the hill, and we all lived down below. We called her 'The Queen." I don't think she associated with common people."[34]

A little more information about Mona in the Gorge is in an autobiography by Lois Davis Plotts, who was born on a ranch near Columbus on the Columbia River, the nearest town to the site where Sam Hill would build his Maryhill chateau and eventually establish his Maryhill community. Lois married Henry Davis, Sam's cousin, in September 1920 in Columbus. Through Henry she knew Sam, but she never met Mona. She would have been well aware of Mona's property, however, as Henry Davis sold it to Sam in 1917.

In her self-published, 1978 book, entitled *Maryhill, Sam Hill and Me*, Mrs. Plotts writes that she first heard about Mona "in a letter from a woman who was slightly acquainted with her in 1930." The letter, reproduced in the book, says, in part:

> *"Mona Bell Hill was the next best thing to a movie star—a real live mistress who lived in a $50,000 home built for her by Sam Hill. The site afforded a beautiful view of the Columbia River and she seemed to live there mostly alone with her small son, Sammy. A Japanese gardener attended the grounds and neighbor ladies reported in scandalized tones that Mrs. Hill often directed his activities in her night gown.*
>
> *"How the neighbor ladies determined this is interesting for the house was secluded and few of the ladies called upon Mona. In fact, she did not mix much with the residents at Bonneville, probably by her own choice.*
>
> *"But this was in 1930 and any deviation from the moral norm was questionable. No one bought the story that she married one of Sam's Seattle cousins and that Sammy was born of that union. Red-haired, stocky and about two-and-a-half years old, he did look very much like Sam, who appeared now and then at Bonneville. Mona Bell herself was a pleasant woman, handsome rather than pretty. She was well-dressed in casual clothes that fit the country scene.*
>
> *"The house is gone now ... but Mona is remembered for two things: a recipe for delicious salmon casserole and an unpretty way she begged, pleaded and stormed at Sam on his deathbed, trying to get him to leave more money to her and Sammy.*

The letter is signed, "Sincerely, Mrs. U.W." Mrs. Plotts does not identify her and also does not provide the date of the letter.[35]

Lorena S. Fisher, whose husband, Lawrence, was the first electrical engineer on the Bonneville Dam construction project, recalled Mona as "an interesting and controversial member of the community," who was "gregarious by nature and liked male company but was not very friendly or popular with women." Fisher's gossipy, self-published 1991 memoir, entitled *The Bonneville Dream*, alleges Mona had suitors from the local area who included "a handsome surveyor" and "one of the dashing guards," and that Mona got into a fight with the Bonneville railroad agent, a woman, over the guard. This occurred at "... a well-attended dance in the [Bonneville community] auditorium."[36] She does not say when this occurred.

Mrs. Fisher also recalled Mona's son:

> *"I remember little Sam, a handsome but rather lonely child. He was sitting in his mother's big car one day and Tommy [Lorena's son] and I passed by. He stuck out his hand and said, "Hello, little boy. What's your name?" But Mona Bell just drove away. A Philippine cook, an Indian gardener, and a maid took care of them."*

In hindsight, none of the gossip, inaccurate as it might have been—note the various nationalities of the gardener—surprises Mona's daughter-in-law.

"Mona Bell was a wild woman so I imagine she would be gossiped about," Virginia Hill said. "And you know what? I don't think it would have bothered her at all. She'd get this twinkle in her eye. Whenever something tickled her, she'd get this little twinkle in her eye. She enjoyed upsetting people."

While Mona could be aloof or friendly as she chose, and upset people without concern, she could not control fate, and in February 1931 her world imploded. On the 6th, Oregon Governor Julius Meier invited his long-time friend Sam Hill to address a joint session of the Legislature at the state Capitol in Salem on February 9. Sam had not been feeling well for a couple of months, but he insisted on maintaining his busy work schedule. On Sunday, February 8, he returned to Portland from a trip to New York. His physicians had advised against that trip, and also recommended that he cancel the Salem speech, but Sam was insistent. The topic, regulation of trucks to protect paved highways, was important to him and he planned to make a similar speech in Olympia later the same week.

On Monday, however, his condition had so worsened that he went to St. Vincent's Hospital, where he was admitted with acute abdominal pain. He had surgery and, after 10 days, improved, but then worsened rapidly. His son, James, came from Boston by airplane; Edgar Hill rushed from Seattle. On the evening of February 26, those two and W.F. Turner, president of the Spokane, Portland & Seattle Railway, were at Sam's bedside when he died. The official cause was an abscess of the lesser peritoneal cavity, which ruptured into his stomach and caused internal hemorrhaging. His biographer, John Tuhy, a Portland physician, speculated the abscess may have been related to acute pancreatitis, a perforated duodenal ulcer, or some other intestinal lesion.[37]

Mona tried to see him but could not get into his room—the same room where Edgar, her nominal husband, maintained a vigil with James Hill and W.F. Turner. It isn't clear how she knew Sam was ill or found out where he was hospitalized, but his illness and hospitalization were reported in the newspapers and he may have stopped to see her in the Gorge on his return from New York.

When she was refused admission as herself, she tried again dressed as a nurse, was discovered and ejected, and then again as janitor. This time she got into the room, but whether she was able to talk to Sam, and whether he was alert at that point, is not clear today, despite the gossip at Bonneville that she begged for money.

"She never talked about her relationship with Sam, at least not very much," Virginia Hill said. "The only thing she did talk about was when he died. She talked about how she disguised herself and went into the hospital, and was discovered and thrown out."

But while she was there, Mona, who hid in a closet to avoid detection, at least got to look at Sam before he died. In his biography of Sam, Tuhy reports an unconfirmed story—perhaps from Lois Davis Plotts' memoir—that Mona wanted to talk Sam into leaving her something in his will. Her son, Sam B. Hill, said that probably was not true.

Virginia Hill said she thought Mona's primary motivation was love, but that it would not have been out of character for Mona to raise the issue of inheritance, either. "I think she was so protective of him that she just wanted to see him when he was so ill. But it's possible that she went to try to get him to leave her something in his will. She was a smart woman," she said.

The death of the iconic Sam Hill was widely reported in the press. An article in the *Seattle Post-Intelligencer* for Saturday, February 27, called Sam "a widely known humanitarian," adding:

> *"Samuel Hill's life was a perpetual contradiction of the adage that a Jack of all trades is good at none. He tried his hand at everything—and invariably with notable success. He was a lawyer, a road builder, a financier, a diplomat, a railway operator, a real estate dealer in the course of his crowded career—and at each of these he made a mark. But it is as a friend of humanity that he will be longest remembered — an unpaid, public servant who gave bounteously of his genius and his energy for the common benefit of mankind."*[38]

Sam had signed his will in November 1930. A Minneapolis newspaper reported Sam's holdings were worth about $500,000—an amount many considered surprisingly low because of his long involvement in many profitable business enterprises. The will provided for funeral expenses and a crypt, eventually placed near the Stonehenge memorial. He left nothing to his wife because of her large inheritance from her father, but Sam included a provision that if that money were to run out, his estate should provide her $1,000 a month, as he had done ever since they were married. The will provided James an annual income of $12,000; the estate would pay for the care of Sam's invalid daughter; Edgar received a house at Blaine and a $25,000 share in Ye Olde English Restaurant Company; Maryhill Museum received half of the estate plus the land and unfinished chateau. There was more, including instructions for the disposition of Sam's house in Seattle, which he previously conveyed to his investment business, United States Trust Company.

The will does not mention Sam's mistresses or his three children by those women, as Sam had established their generous trust funds separately. The trust for Mona and her baby stipulated that she would receive the interest from a principal amount of $60,000.[39]

Sam's will was not acceptable to his wife, Mary, and son, James. Perhaps because of the trust funds for the children or perhaps because

Mary and James did not feel properly compensated in the will, they fought it in court. Mary hired a Seattle attorney to file a petition asking the King County Probate Court to declare Sam's assets as community property because her marriage to Sam never was annulled and they never divorced. James had the same attorney file a petition questioning the legality of the bequest to the museum. The discussions among attorneys lasted five years, until 1936, finally resulting in a settlement that satisfied James and his mother, who each received cash payments plus partial ownership of timberlands in Lewis County, Washington.[40]

Sam's death left Mona more alone than ever on her hilltop. The father of her then three-year-old son had left her a magnificent home in the Columbia River Gorge and a decent sum of regular income through the trust. Despite this largess, though, he also had let her know at some time before he died that while he loved her, he loved another woman even more.

Virginia Hill recalls Mona telling her the story.

"The only thing she said about their being together was about one time when they were walking on a beach, I don't know where, and he told her he was in love," Virginia said. "And she said she felt so good to be with him, and that she loved him so much. And then he said, 'but I am in love with a queen.' He meant Queen Marie. Mona Bell was devastated. He was a real womanizer, you know."

Regardless, Virginia said, "She certainly loved him. He was the love of her life."

Imagine Mona's dismay over Sam's death. The man she loved, the father of her child, the man who had married her to his cousin to legitimize the boy with the Hill name, and who also had admitted he was in love with another woman—a European queen, no less—was gone. It was 1931. In Oregon, as across the country, unemployment was high, and the nation struggled to rebuild from the economic devastation of the Great Depression.

The election of President Franklin D. Roosevelt in 1932 would bring a new focus on labor, as opposed to business, and his New Deal would spur government investments in public works projects. Soon hundreds, then thousands, of workers would arrive on the riverfront below Mona's home to build one of America's largest hydroelectric dams, a project of great importance to Roosevelt.

"Right after his inauguration, Roosevelt came to Oregon, and I have a vague feeling he came to our house," Sam B. Hill recalled. "I think I remember my mother telling me that. She hated him. She felt he was responsible for taking her home."

CHAPTER 5

Bonneville Dam

ROUND THE YEAR 1700, OR PERHAPS AS MANY AS 600 YEARS EARLIER, A MOUNTAIN ON THE NORTH SIDE OF THE COLUMBIA RIVER ABOUT 40 MILES UPSTREAM FROM THE PORTLAND/VANCOUVER AREA COLLAPSED, probably as the result of an earthquake, and spilled nearly a cubic mile of rock and debris to the south over an area of about 14 square miles. This enormous landslide blocked the Columbia River in the area of the present-day Bridge of the Gods, at Cascade Locks, Oregon, and Stevenson, Washington.

The Cascade Landslide pushed the river channel south a mile, a feature still plainly evident from the air. The river backed up behind the blockage for a distance of about 200 miles but eventually broke through, possibly creating a natural bridge—the mythical Bridge of the Gods—but certainly creating a seven-mile stretch of boulder-strewn white water that came to be known as the Cascades Rapids. The Cascades Rapids posed the last, and one of the most treacherous, obstacles to wagon-train pioneers of the mid-19th Century who were forced to either load their belongings onto barges at The Dalles for the wild ride down the river or face the arduous trek around Mount Hood on the Barlow Trail. Eventually, portage railroads were constructed so that those who could afford the portage fees could avoid the dangerous rapids. The first was on the Oregon side, completed in 1851. It consisted of a single, mule-drawn cart on rails. By 1862, railroad portages were operating on both shores of the Columbia River. The federal government began constructing locks at the Cascades to facilitate river traffic in 1878; the locks were completed in 1896.

In the late 1800s, as electric power proliferated in American cities, engineers began experimenting with generators driven by the power of falling water. The first hydroelectric generator coupled to a water-powered turbine lit a theater and storefront arc bulbs in Grand Rapids, Michigan, in 1880. Soon, hydroelectric plants using a similar technology were operating in many cities across the country, including Spokane in

1885, and Portland in 1889. In both cities, the small hydropower plants provided electricity for street lights. A dam on the Willamette River at Oregon City provided power for street lights in downtown Portland.

For more than 100 years, the Cascades Rapids were little more than a geographic place of interest and a difficult stretch of river, first for pioneers and later for steamboats. But the Cascades attracted new attention in the early part of the 20th Century when the federal government began to take an interest in developing large-scale water projects on the nation's largest rivers, including the Columbia and Snake, for hydropower, navigation, irrigation, and flood control. Privately owned electric utilities also were interested in developing rivers for hydropower.

Soon a critical disagreement developed: Who should control the public waterways—privately owned electric utilities that took the risks of investing in dam construction to generate power for their customers, or the government, which owned the water on behalf of all citizens and had the financial resources, if not the power-generating experience, to build dams?

Privately owned electric utilities and their parent corporations fiercely opposed federal control of water power developments. Private businesses already controlled the generation and distribution of electricity, and they wanted to expand their holdings to include dams. Others warned about the dangers of monopoly businesses that could control access to electricity and set its cost. In many areas of the country, electricity largely was unavailable outside of urban areas because it was not cost-effective for utilities to extend their lines to rural areas for the benefit of small numbers of customers.

In this important battle, the anti-monopolists had two formidable allies: Theodore Roosevelt, president of the United States from 1901-1909, and Gifford Pinchot, chief forester of the U.S. Forest Service at that time. Neither was an advocate of public power, but both opposed monopolies and advocated conservation of natural resources. Pinchot, for whom a national forest in southwest Washington is named, was president of the National Conservation Association from 1910, when he left the Forest Service, to 1923, when he was elected governor of Pennsylvania.

Roosevelt embraced the concept of multiple-purpose dams that would create slackwater for navigation, control flooding, and generate hydropower. In 1906, and again in 1910 after Roosevelt left office, the General Dam Acts authorized the federal government to license water power dams on navigable rivers. Water power became a national issue under Roosevelt. In 1907, he created the Inland Waterways Commission to study development of the nation's rivers. In February 1908, the Commission delivered its preliminary report to Congress. The report declared rivers are assets of the people, warned about monopolies taking over river development, and endorsed multiple-purpose development of rivers. According to the report:

> *Our river systems are better adapted to the needs of the people than those of any other country . . . Yet the rivers of no other civilized country are so poorly developed, so little used, or play so small a part in the industrial life of the nation as those of the United States. It is poor business to develop a river for navigation in such a way as to prevent its use for power, when by a little foresight it could be made to serve both purposes. We cannot afford needlessly to sacrifice power to irrigation, or irrigation to domestic water supply, when by taking thought we may have all three. Every stream should be used to the utmost.*

At the same time, state agencies and local groups of irrigators and community boosters also were investigating the potential of the Columbia for multiple purposes—navigation, hydropower, and irrigation. Irrigation was the primary interest in Washington, where the river flowed past hundreds of square miles of agricultural land in the central part of the state that could be made more productive with Columbia River water. In Oregon, the primary concern was providing hydropower to the Portland area.

One of the earliest reconnaissance reports on potential Columbia River dam sites was prepared for the office of the Oregon State Engineer by L.F. Harza of Portland and published in 1916. According to the report, "For years we have talked in generalities of the great water power possibilities of Oregon and of the Columbia River basin.

Little thought has been given to the study of any particular project, or how the power of that project could be utilized." But that year, 1916, two potential projects were studied thoroughly, one at The Dalles and the other at Bonneville. According to the report:

> "... the most logical project to suggest for early construction is at Bonneville, on the Columbia River. Because of its proximity to Portland, the metropolis of Oregon, its location at the head of tide water, and its effect on navigation of the Columbia River as far as The Dalles, where over 1,000,000 electrical horsepower can be had in projects of various sizes, and the necessity for overcoming the swift water between Bonneville and Cascade Locks before the upper power could be utilized in manufacturing products for world markets, it was thought fitting to investigate this project in some detail."

As well, the river in the area of the Cascades Rapids had only a modest, and relatively stable drop throughout the year—the river-level difference between lowest flows (winter and late summer) and highest flows (spring and early summer) was only seven feet, and this meant that the dam would not have to be designed to handle huge variations in river elevation. At The Dalles, by contrast, the annual variation could be more than 50 feet. A dam there would have to be larger in order to operate efficiently year-round. And developing the Bonneville site first would flood the Cascades rapids, "...providing ocean-draft navigation to The Dalles, thus improving the transportation facilities for industries using power at the latter place," according to the report.

The report concluded that it would be less expensive over the long run to build a small dam at The Dalles and a large dam at Bonneville to accommodate the growing demand for power. And demand growth was inevitable, it seemed, as Portland and the Columbia definitely were in the sites of developers. According to the report, "Promoters of industrial projects have been here in large numbers; they have carefully surveyed the field for their respective industries; they have prepared elaborate prospectuses and presented them with all possible forcefulness ..."

Despite the optimistic tone of the report, the showstopper issue was how much the dam at Bonneville would cost and how it would be financed. Using cost estimates for machinery and excavation from a similar study of the hydropower potential at The Dalles, published serially in 1915 and 1916, Harza estimated the cost of the Bonneville project at $20 million (about $380 million in 2006 dollars). Harza wrote that the cost "...would not seem to be too great to permit the sale of power for prospective chemical service, if financed upon some cheap interest basis, and especially if navigation interests could bear a portion of the expense." With World War I looming, chemical industries needed large amounts of power to make nitrates for explosives. Certainly these industries understood the potential for vast amounts of cheap electricity from the Columbia River. But Harza's report does not name any that had expressed interest in helping to finance such a large project.

In 1916, the question of whether the government—state, federal, or both—or business should finance big, multiple-purpose dams was hardly settled. Four years later, however, Congress resolved the matter in the Federal Water Power Act of 1920 without really declaring a winner. Large dams could be built either by the government or by businesses, but a new federal commission would oversee the construction of privately financed dams to ensure they were operated in the public interest. Following on the theme of the earlier General Dam Acts, the new law created the Federal Power Commission to license dams built by privately owned companies and also to regulate interstate sales of electricity, an important issue at the time.

Meanwhile, at the national level, Franklin D. Roosevelt, like his cousin Theodore, supported conservation of natural resources and development of water power on the nation's rivers. In 1920, when he was campaigning for the vice presidency, Franklin Roosevelt arrived in Portland after traveling down the Columbia River Gorge. The river made an impression, as he noted in a speech:

> "When you cross the Mountain States and that portion of the Coast States that lies well back from the ocean, you are impressed by those great stretches of physical territory now practically unused but destined some day to contain the homes of thousands

and hundreds of thousands of citizens like us, a territory to be developed by the Nation and for the Nation. As we were coming down the river today, I could not help thinking, as everyone does, of all that water running unchecked down to the sea."

Roosevelt's impressions of the Columbia mirrored a growing national interest in developing the untapped potential of the nation's rivers. In 1925, Congress authorized the Army Engineers and the Federal Power Commission to jointly:

" . . .prepare and submit to Congress an estimate of the cost of making such examinations, surveys or other investigations. . . of those navigable streams of the United States and their tributaries . . . with a view to the formulation of general plans for the most effective improvement of such streams for the purposes of navigation and prosecution of such improvement in combination with the most efficient development of the potential water power, the control of floods and the needs of irrigation."

The response, published as House Document 308 on April 12, 1926, featured the Columbia prominently. This and subsequent "308 reports" were the basic planning documents for the development of navigation, flood control, irrigation, and hydropower in the Columbia River Basin.

In the 1926 report, the Secretary of War provided cost estimates and recommended surveys of potential dam sites, which were authorized the following year in the River and Harbor Act of 1927. The subsequent surveys were completed in 1932 and presented to Congress on March 29 of that year. Entitled, "Columbia River and Minor Tributaries," the survey and report totaled 1,845 pages. The report, known also as House Document 103, proposed a plan for building eight dams on the Columbia, with Grand Coulee, 596 river miles inland from the ocean, and Bonneville, at river mile 140, as the two "bookends." The plan also envisioned water storage dams farther upstream on Columbia tributaries, including Hungry Horse Dam in western Montana. The Army Engineers expanded the plan to 10 dams on the Columbia. All of these dams, consistent with congressional direction in 1925, were to be built for the purpose of "improving the Columbia River and minor tributaries for the purposes of navigation and efficient development of water-power, the control of floods and the needs of irrigation."

The report declared that the Columbia had the potential to be "the greatest system for water power to be found anywhere in the United States" and that the river could be controlled and managed as one system. It would be an expensive undertaking to build the 10 dams envisioned in the report, more than any other multiple-purpose dam development on a single river system. Ten dams would generate much more electricity than could be used at the time, but the development was viewed as a sort of self-fulfilling prophecy—as the dams were built and electricity became available, demand from new industries and consumers would materialize to take the power.

Through the 1920s, interest remained strong in Oregon for a dam in the area of the Cascades Rapids. Portland General Electric studied a potential site but decided the anticipated cost—$30 million—was too high for a privately owned business. A dam big enough to cross the Columbia likely could be built only by government.

The closest city to the Cascades Rapids was Cascade Locks, Oregon. Bonneville, Oregon, about five miles downstream near the end of the rapids, was an unincorporated hamlet on one of the few flat areas with easy river access in the area. It consisted of a few homes and businesses, including a restaurant, tavern, campground, and train station.

Finding a workable site for a dam at or near Bonneville proved vexing. The Army Engineers studied several possible sites, but the Cascade landslide added a layer of complexity to the already tortured geology of the Columbia River Gorge. The Gorge was formed during the Miocene era (12-17 million years ago) and the Pleistocene era (700,000-2 million years ago), when the Cascade Mountains rose in a series of volcanic eruptions. At the time, the river entered the Pacific 100 miles or so south of its present course, but as the mountains and surrounding areas rose, the river found a new route to the sea and slowly eroded the Gorge. At the end of the last ice age about 14,000-20,000 years ago, repeated floods—perhaps as many as 2,000—crashed through the Gorge when the ice dam holding back the melt water of Lake Missoula, in present-day western Montana, repeatedly gave way and reformed. In the Gorge, the floods exposed multiple layers of lava—21 flows poured through the Gorge during the Miocene era alone.

Volcanism, flooding, the Cascades Landslide, and thousands of years of sediment transport left the river with a bed that was solid rock in some places, fractured rock in others, and deeply layered loose rock and sand in still others. In short, finding a solid place to anchor a large dam was extremely difficult.

A site near Warrendale, several miles downriver from Bonneville, looked promising—it was the Army's preferred location in the 308 Report—but because its subsurface was largely sand and gravel, Congress ordered further studies. These disclosed two sites farther upstream with subsurface rock formations. The Warrendale site was rejected in favor of the two upriver finalists, and additional studies showed that one of them, the Bonneville site, was the best. Detailed survey work began in November 1933 at the north end of Bradford Island but was quickly halted by a flood the following month. Meanwhile, a site with even more substantial bedrock was discovered about 2,000 feet downstream. In March 1934, this site became the preferred location for the big dam.

Corps of Engineers historian William J. Willingham writes: "At this spot, two basalt intrusions or uplifts in the bedrock provided ideal foundations for the dam, powerhouse, and lock. Upstream and downstream from these ledges, bedrock dropped off precipitously. The new location also meant a savings of $3 million and shortening of the construction time by one work season."[41]

This ideal protrusion of bedrock was immediately below Mona Bell Hill's mansion.

CHAPTER 6

The Battle

*R*EAL ESTATE RECORDS OF THE PORTLAND DISTRICT OF THE U.S. ARMY CORPS OF ENGINEERS DON'T INDICATE WHEN THE WAR DEPARTMENT FIRST CONTACTED MONA ABOUT ACQUIRING HER PROPERTY AND HOME for the Bonneville Dam construction project. But with the initial work in the river beginning in November 1933 and then moving half a mile downriver the following March, it is likely that War Department real estate specialists were talking to Mona sometime in late 1933, and possibly earlier—five years or fewer after the house was built.

The War Department offered $25,600 for her property; Mona asked for $100,000, and there the negotiations stalemated.[42] There was no further progress through the winter. Just one month before work began at the final location of the dam, the government filed a petition for condemnation in U.S. District Court in Portland. In all, the government condemned 36 pieces of property for the Bonneville Project, but this was the only condemnation that went to trial.

The petition, filed on Feb. 8, was granted the following day, Feb. 9, 1934. The order granted the government immediate possession, and crews began clearing the riverfront portion of Mona's property in preparation for construction of a small city for Bonneville Project workers. This included an administration building, auditorium, and 20 two-story, Colonial revival-style houses neatly situated on pleasant curving streets. These houses, intended for War Department employees, were in addition to the dormitories already constructed for laborers.

The petition, signed by Carl C. Donaugh, United States Attorney for Oregon, cited the National Industrial Recovery Act of 1933 as justification for the government's condemnation of the house and property to make way for the construction of Bonneville Dam. The petition asks the court to grant the government "immediate possession of the said premises...at a price that the court determines is "reasonable and adequate."[43]

To Mona, this was nothing less than an aggressive, overt, and unnecessary campaign to steal her home and property. Never one to retreat from a fight, particularly in defense of something she held dear, Mona fought back aggressively. She retained Jay Bowerman, a former Oregon state senator and interim governor, to manage her counterattack. Bowerman was one of Portland's most prominent and respected attorneys and a friend of Sam Hill.

In her answer to the government's condemnation petition, Mona rejected the government's contention that her property was needed for the Bonneville project. There was plenty of flat land along the river in that area where the government could build housing for dam workers, she argued, and most of it already was in federal ownership. She submitted copies of her two lease agreements with John Golden Barnett, whose small home stood on a corner of the property at the base of the hill. She asserted that her property was so far removed from the actual construction site of the dam that it could not reasonably be considered necessary for the project. In fact, War Department real estate personnel had told Mona they did not want the hilltop, where her home stood, but only the 12-14 acres of flat land in the northwestern corner of her property, where the government planned to build housing for the construction workers and Army employees.

Her answer made the point that her home had been carefully located to take advantage of the view: "The dwelling house and residence of this defendant, occupied by herself and her minor son, is constructed upon a promontory more than 200 feet high and said house is so constructed as to have an outlook in the immediate foreground over the lower levels of plaintiff's property and over a wide range of vision across and down and upstream along the Gorge of the Columbia."

The 20-room house cost $65,000 to build, Mona's answer asserted, and it contained "furniture and equipment particularly adapted thereto which would have but little value elsewhere." The answer also notes that Mona had a priority water right for the property and house, and that she had constructed an extensive irrigation system for her gardens and landscaped grounds that included "a great number of flowering shrubs and perennial plants," and also a private driveway connecting to the highway "with adequate and convenient turnouts and a turnaround" at the house. The landscaping work, which Mona completed herself, truly was a labor of love on her part. This included removing trees and undergrowth, hauling out large amounts of rock and dirt, and hauling in compost, fertilizer, and hundreds of shrubs and plants.

The answer makes the point that Mona had plans for the property, if not immediately, then in the near future. She had been granted a second water right, which may have been for the house but also may have been for a business she planned along the highway below her house, possibly a new campground. At least 10 years earlier, Sam Lancaster, who was Sam Hill's partner in the construction of the Columbia River Highway, built an auto camp and picnic area called Camp Get-a-Way on the north side of the highway immediately west of the property now owned by Mona. The camp had been destroyed by fire and not rebuilt. A small hotel and mercantile store were located west of the former campground. Clearly, there were business opportunities in the immediate area. If Mona didn't develop her property along the highway, she could lease parcels to others who would.

She also asserted that representatives of the War Department had told her that 21 acres—approximately two-thirds of the property—comprising the southeastern corner that included much of her landscaped yard and gardens, would be offered to the state of Oregon for the purpose of relocating the Columbia River Highway. Her estate included land on both sides of the highway. But employees of the state's Highway Commission had told her there were no plans to widen or relocate the highway across her property at that time. At any rate, the reasonable value of her home and improvements, and the riverfront property in the growing little community of Bonneville, was $100,000, she claimed.

There was more, and this was personal: She claimed the War Department had knowingly vandalized her property and burglarized her home while she was traveling in late 1933. She alleged the War Department "cut, tore down, and destroyed a large amount of valuable trees, flowering shrubs, and other shrubs and flowering bushes ... and contrary to defendants' directions and instructions ... went upon and in and through defendant's house and through her private bedroom." She estimated the damage at $5,000. She had demanded compensation, but none was paid.

The government fired back with predictable denials. In his reply brief, U.S. Attorney Carl Donaugh denied that Mona had signed "true and genuine leases" with John Barnett. The government also asserted that Barnett had not agreed to pay her to lease the property. The reply brief referred to "the pretended leases."

This was all legal posturing, of course, and Mona's attorney later would enter the signed leases as evidence in the trial in support of her claim. This was not a minor point of contention, as her co-defendant Barnett, a businessman who lived in Portland, had leased two sizable tracts along the south side of the Columbia River Highway from Mona—one was 690 feet long by 100 feet deep, and the other was 200 feet by 200 feet—for a total of $8,000 over five years, beginning in late 1933. The lease for the larger parcel was dated Dec. 2, 1933, and for the smaller one, Oct. 26, 1933. Barnett then either had improved the land or sub-leased to others who improved it, or both, as at the trial he claimed the value of the two leases to him totaled $31,200 over the five-year period.

Donaugh also disputed Mona's claim that the government really only needed the level ground near the river, comprising 12-14 acres, for the Bonneville project and not her entire parcel including the hilltop and house. He did not say why. "The Secretary of War has determined that it is advantageous to, and necessary for, the Government of the United States to acquire all the lands described in the petition herein," according to the reply brief.

And in what must have been, to Mona, the most stinging rebuke, the government's reply denied that Mona's home had 20 rooms or that Mona had spent $65,000 on it and the landscaping. The government claimed Mona spent no more than $21,150 and that she had recovered $9,784 "... from building contractors and bondsmen ..." leaving her net investment in the house and property $10,365.96. The brief does not explain how or why Mona recovered money from building contractors. The government claimed that the fair market value was $25,600 and also denied that Mona was entitled to interest on the value of the property since February, when the court granted the initial condemnation order. The reply brief does not address Mona's complaint that her land already was being cleared or that government employees had burglarized her home.

The battle lines now were set.

The matter proceeded to trial in April 1934, but already had attracted press attention two months before. On Saturday, February 10, 1934, the day after Judge John H. McNary granted the government's petition for condemnation, *The Oregonian* reported on the order, but not prominently. In fact, the initial story about the government seizing an apparently substantial private home to make way for the Portland area's biggest federal public works project warranted no more than Page 6, and that in a brief article toward the bottom of the page under two others in the same column entitled, "Muffins One Way of Using Small Grain," and "Flea Circus Due for Annual Tour." The five-inch article was headlined, "Government Gets Land; Court Orders Conveyance at Bonneville." Mona is identified as Mrs. E. Bell Hill.

According to the article, the federal government sought the land because it was in the area of the Bonneville construction project and "because an agreement could not be reached between the government and Mrs. Hill." The article continues:

> *"Mrs. Hill asked approximately $100,000 for the tract and the government was willing to pay approximately $30,000, it is understood. Mrs. Hill holds, according to reports, that she had built her home on the property and has planted the grounds with trees and shrubs which she imported from many parts of the world."*

John Golden Barnett is identified as a co-defendant because of his leases.

No further coverage of the dispute was in any of Portland's three major daily newspapers—the others were *The Oregon Daily Journal* and *The Portland Evening-Telegram*—until the trial began four months later.

Unfortunately, transcripts of the two trials—the initial one in 1934 and a retrial in 1935—could not be located. However, events of the trials can be pieced together from newspaper accounts.

On June 22, 1934, *The Oregonian* reported on the opening of the initial trial in an article headlined, "Dam Site Trial Starts; Jurors

Will Set Price on E. Bell Hill Property; Government Launches First Condemnation Action in Area of Bonneville." The jurors included a hardware salesman, an orderly at St. Vincent's Hospital, an accountant, a carpenter, and interestingly, a man identified as Harry Whitney. There is no further identification, but the name is similar to that of one of Portland's best-known architects at the time, Harrison Whitney, a partner in the firm of Sutton, Whitney, and Aandahl. An architect, particularly one of Whitney's standing in Portland, could have been an important ally for Mona's claim that the house was unique and valuable.

The jury of 12 men "will set a price which the government must pay for Mrs. Hill's land, which federal officials took over last February," according to the article, which accurately reported, compared to the February article, that the government offered $25,600 and Mona "is demanding $100,000." Both were substantial sums in 1934. The trial was about more than the loss of a magnificent home. It was about big money.

After opening statements by Asst. U.S. Attorney John W. McCulloch, Bowerman, and Barnett's attorney, Charles W. Erskine, court was recessed and the jurors were taken to view the property. This was the government's idea, and in hindsight it would seem to have been a bad one. It was June. Some of the flowering shrubs likely were in bloom; the home would have been, presumably, as spotless and well-kept as the impeccable grounds; and to tour such a grand place with its stunning views up and down the Gorge at a time of the year when all around is lush green and the air is summery warm, could only have left a favorable impression. It was a pleasant day, with a trace of rain in Portland and a high temperature of 68 degrees but sunny skies in the Columbia River Gorge, where the high was 69 in Hood River. There is no press account of the jurors' visit.

The article about the first day of the trial mentions Sam Hill, Mona, and her son, but doesn't overtly connect the three despite their names: "Mrs. Hill, whose 6-year-old son is named for the late Sam Hill, one of the locators of the Columbia River Highway, builder of the Maryhill estate on the Washington side of the river, says her property was selected personally by Mr. Hill as one of the greatest viewpoints

An undated photo of a painting of Mona in the nude.

Frances Bell, Mona's sister, at the family home in Grand Forks, North Dakota. The photo is undated but probably was taken in the late 1920s.

Mona with her pet deer outside the original log cabin on her Dunbar Lake property. The photo is undated, but the cabin was struck by lightning and destroyed in the late 1930s.

This undated photo shows Mona and Edgar Hill at a beach, possibly somewhere on the Oregon or Washington coast. It is the only known photo of Mona and Edgar.

Mona, left, her mother, Esther, and Esther's sister, Mary, in the basement of Esther's home in Grand Forks, N.D., around 1940. Mona shot the cheetah whose skin is on the faux-log wall.

The Columbia River Gorge, looking east from the Portland Women's Forum Park. Beacon Rock is in the distance.

The view looking down from Mona's hilltop includes the navigation lock at Bonneville Dam. Shrubbery in the foreground, including arborvitae, could have been planted by Mona.

Viewed from Bradford Island, Mona's hilltop is on the south side of the navigation lock on the south, or Oregon, side of Bonneville Dam. In this photo, Mona's mansion stood on the right, or west, side of the hill. The visible northern flank was blasted away when the Union Pacific Railroad tracks were relocated.

Mona's mansion in 1940, five years after Mona was evicted. The Army Engineers remodeled the home into two apartments, one upstairs and the other on the main floor.

The mansion as it appeared from the Bonneville community during construction of the dam. The photo is dated March 1935; Mona was evicted in July.

This piece of the foundation of Mona's mansion shows a remnant of the swirled, California-style heavy stucco finish on the exterior.

The auditorium and community center at Bonneville Dam, which once served the community of construction workers, engineers, and others who built the dam, stands on what was Mona's property. The hilltop where her mansion stood is directly behind the building.

6441 P.W.A., War, Rivers and Harbors, 1933-1935. (Bonneville Power and Navigation projects.) 32nd Contract W-698eng.-672. May 18, 1935. Camera Site: Northeast end of fish hatchery. Exposure: East. New civic auditorium.

This May 1935 photo, taken two months before Mona was evicted, shows the newly completed auditorium and community center. Mona's mansion is at the top of the photo.

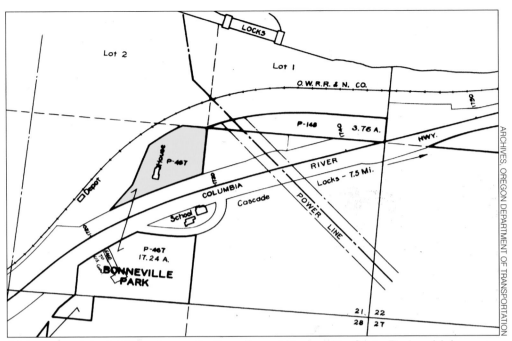

This map, dated 1961, shows the location of Bonneville State Park, which never was developed. The park totaled 51.05 acres in five unconnected parcels. The 17.42-acre parcel in the middle of the map once was part of Mona's property. The identified "house" in the northern part of the parcel is Mona's mansion.

This Oregon State Highway document records the transfer of the deed to Mona's property from the War Department to the State of Oregon in January 1945. According to the document, the deed was sent to Oregon Parks Commission Director Samuel Boardman, ending eight years of effort by the state to acquire the property.

Construction of Interstate 84, a widening and realigning of the old Columbia River Highway, carved away the south side of the hill. Mona's mansion stood at the left, (west), side of the hill in this view, taken from the Tooth Rock Trailhead parking lot.

The envelope of a letter Mona sent to her sister, Frances, from Beirut—on stationery from a Cairo Hotel. The letter is undated, but the postmark appears to be March 28, 1936, and the arrival stamp in Grand Forks, April 17. Mona tells Frances to expect a shipment of rugs and brass.

Mar. 31 – 75

From the desk of
MONA BELL HILL
28458 East
WORCESTER
SUN CITY – Cal –

Bonnie dear:–
So sorry to hear of your loss but I know you'll never be sorry of all the pleasure + comfort you have given to your dear mother that loves you so much — If you ever have any friends coming down this way I'll be glad to fill their ear with bedding + articles you could

use – I could furnish them with bed + food while they were here but no service at 85 I can't take care of myself + no help available –
I am enclosing a check for $100 + hope that will help a little
    Love
       your
    aunt Mona

Six years before she died, Mona wrote to her niece after Frances, Mona's sister, died. Mona complained of having no one to help her, which was not true.

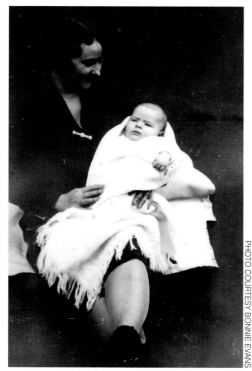

Mona with Sam, born in 1928.

A young Sam B. Hill on horseback. The photo has no identifying information, but most likely it was taken at one of the many boarding schools he attended. Sam loved horses.

Sam B. Hill on a vacation to Alaska in the mid 1950s.

Sam in 1984 with daughter, Paula, at her wedding.

The author at Mona's grave in the Forest Lawn Hollywood Hills Cemetery. The grave is only marked by metal disks at each of the four corners that identify Grave 6129.

Tony Hill and his grandmother, Virginia Hill, in Virginia's living room with two of Mona's unusual souvenirs from her travels—a spear and a shield.

In her home in the Los Angeles area, Virginia Hill keeps many mementos of her mother in law, including Mona's custom-made dining room table, an engraved ivory cigarette holder, glassware, silverware, candlesticks, and decorative plates.

Virginia Hill wears a large ring acquired by Mona on her international travels (stone in ring and pendant is onyx).

Mona had a large collection of jewelry, including many pieces that she purchased on her world travels. The carved pendant inlaid with silver and mother of pearl, and the silver bracelets and pendant are shown on one of Mona's red satin pillows.

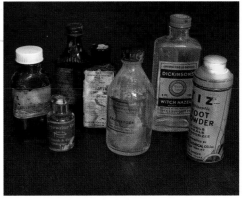

When Mona left her mansion in the Columbia River Gorge, she packed everything, including these medicine bottles and a can of foot powder. Decades later, Virginia Hill found these in a box that had not been opened since Mona packed it in 1935.

Mona's yellow glassware is in Virginia Hill's home today.

This is the beaded leather apron Mona acquired on a safari in Kenya, probably in 1936. She told her family she traded her bloomers for the apron, which was being worn by a woman Mona met in a rural area. Mona said the woman wanted her bloomers. Mona agreed, but because of her modesty the exchange was effected behind a large rock.

Mona's custom-built hutch, which matches the dining room table, was modeled after furniture Mona saw in a monastery in France. The hutch and table are in the dining room of Virginia Hill's home.

A colorful bowl Mona acquired is now on display in Virginia Hill's living room.

A wood carving of a head is on a wall of Virginia Hill's office.

Mona collected knives on her world travels. These are among her collection. While not particularly valuable, they are unusual.

This is the cabin Mona built on the shore of Dunbar Lake, in north-central Minnesota, about 50 miles northeast of Bemidji, in the late 1930s. It was unusual, as it was several small cabins joined together. Mona built it after the original log home on the property was struck by lightning and burned to the ground. Ironically, in 1982, Mona's cabin was struck by lightning and destroyed.

Tony Hill, Sam Hill's great grandson, lives in Florida. He holds the framed photo of his great grandfather that Mona kept with her until she died.

PHOTO: JOHN C. HARRISON

on the river." The article says that while the defense "will place a high value" on the landscaping, "the government contends that the property has been allowed to deteriorate and that the price it offered was a fair valuation."

Interesting as the events may be in hindsight, with the tacit implication of a relationship between Mona and Sam Hill—he personally selected the site of the home where she lived with her son, who is named after Sam and who was born three years before Sam died—any gossip was left unreported. Nor was the opening of the trial important enough to garner prominent attention among the panoply of daily news. It was an inside story again, this time on Page 7.

The trial opened on a Thursday. On Friday, the government and defense put their witnesses on the stand to testify about their appraisals of the property. Three government witnesses placed the value of the place within $1,000 of the government's offer. The *Journal* reported that Bowerman's associate, John Collier, was "relentless" in his cross-examination. He succeeded in getting one government witness, realtor Henry Reed, who had appraised properties for the War Department in the past, to admit that he thought he might be called as a witness in the trial after he appraised the property at $27,500 on May 23. He insisted he had not seen the newspaper stories in February that quoted the government's $25,600 offer. The jurors, the *Journal* reported, "tittered." Collier also raised questions about the credibility of another government witness, Don E. Meldrum, a civil engineer in the land section of the Army engineers, who admitted during what the *Journal* called "the crossfire" in court that he had "been employed from 1903 to 1930 buying land for corporations at the lowest possible prices." Despite the fact that the two leases for parts of Mona's property would pay her $13,000 over five years, Meldrum said he did not consider this to increase the value of the property because he did not believe the leases were genuine. Coincidentally, neither did the government.

The story in *The Oregonian* the next morning, Saturday, June 23, focused on Mona's testimony, which must have come after the deadline for the *Journal*, an evening paper, as it was riveting She told the court the home had either 17 or 20 rooms, she wasn't sure precisely, but at any rate it was more than the 12 claimed by the government. She said the home was "surrounded by thousands of plants and shrubs in rock gardens, and the estate is partly covered with natural forest." She said she had imported rare tree peonies from China and Japan that cost more than $500 ($7,800 in 2008 dollars) and had been given 14 rhododendron plants from India that were so rare she could not place a value on them. According to the story: "Questioned about the Indian rhododendrons by her counsel, Jay Bowerman, Mrs. Hill wiped her eyes with a handkerchief and sobbed, 'I'd rather let the government take them than place a value on them.'" The article reported that Mona asked Judge McNary to allow her to take the rhododendrons and tree peonies from the property regardless of the eventual verdict of the jury, but he refused, saying that the matter before the court was the value of the property. While the plants could be used to value the property, it was not up to the jury to determine whether they could be removed, McNary ruled.

Bowerman introduced 21 exhibits into evidence, including 10 photographs of the property, five maps to accompany the defense witness appraisals, copies of the two leases with John Golden Barnett and copies of checks to prove his payments, a price list for the tree peonies, a list of all of the shrubbery, and other documents including Mona's water right permit. Bowerman called his own expert appraisers, including landscape architect George Otten, who estimated the value of the landscaping alone at $12,000, and Amedee H. Smith, a real estate expert and former chairman of the Multnomah County Board of Commissioners, who placed the market value of the property at $110,000 to $125,000. He also called Max W. Lorenz, whose construction company, Lorenz Bros., apparently built the mansion. The firm also coordinated construction of Timberline Lodge and built the Gorge estate of Julius Meier, the Portland department store entrepreneur who was the governor of Oregon at the time. Meier's estate, called Menucha, is about 18 miles downriver from Mona's hilltop. Lorenz testified that the construction cost of Mona's home was $17,000, the equivalent of about $270,000 in 2008 dollars.

Monday, June 26, was the highlight of the trial, at least in terms of the star power of the witnesses. Governor Meier, who was a friend of Sam, traveled north from Salem to testify on Mona's behalf. Even so, the story in *The Oregonian* only warranted Page 4, but Meier didn't disappoint. He supported Mona's claim that her estate easily was worth $100,000.

"I have always thought that my property was about the best site [in the Gorge]," the Governor said. "I believe the Hill site has a little bit over mine. Of course, I am not saying anything disparaging about mine, because I may want to sell it sometime."

The governor estimated the value of what the newspaper called "the Hill estate" was "in excess of $100,000," and that its primary value was as a country home and view site. According to the article, "The fact that a portion of the property is leased would increase its value, [Meier] stated upon cross-examination, after he had been informed of the lease by government counsel. 'The property must have a value over and above what I thought of when I sat down here,' he said." Other defense witnesses also testified the estate was worth $100,000 or more, including Dorr Keasey, president of Keasey, Hurley & Keady, Inc., a Portland real estate firm that specialized at the time in selling land for industrial developments near Bonneville Dam and advertised itself as "owners and operators of the North Bonneville town site" on the Washington side of the dam. Keasey's estimate: $112,100.

Amedee M. Smith, the real estate expert and former chairman of the Board of Multnomah County Commissioners, was recalled to the witness stand. The previous Friday he had estimated the value of Mona's estate at $110,000 to $125,000. On Monday the government attorneys questioned him about a letter he wrote in October 1933. In the letter, to a consulting engineer named D.C. Henny, Smith wrote that he had known the country around Bonneville since childhood and that "at no time in all the history of that section has any of the lowlands along the river been worth to exceed $30 an acre." He went on to write that even with the construction of the dam, the lowlands would not bring more than $50 an acre except perhaps if a parcel had some elevation and offered views of the river.

But if the government's intention was to use the letter to cast doubt in the jurors' minds about the actual value of the estate, the attempt failed. Under questioning by Mona's attorneys, Smith clarified that the letter referred to land on the Washington side of the river, not the Oregon side. Another Portland real estate expert, Allison H. Dean, president of Allison Dean Company, had the highest estimated value: $135,166 ($2.1 million in 2008 dollars).

Mona also was recalled to the witness stand. Her testimony was not recorded in press accounts, but another defense witness, Portland landscape architect George Otten, placed the value of the roads and gardens on the estate at $12,000 ($186,200 in 2008 dollars).

The trial lasted through Wednesday, June 27; the jury deliberated until Saturday the 30th and handed up its decision: Mona deserved $75,000 plus interest at 6 percent from Feb. 9, the day Judge McNary signed the condemnation order. The jury awarded John G. Barnett $7,000 for the value of his two leases and $485 to the West Coast Power Company for the value of its right-of-way for electricity lines across the property. The *Journal* reported the verdict in a brief article— finally on Page 1—the same day, June 30. *The Oregonian* erroneously summed these amounts and reported that the jury awarded Mona a total of $82,485.

It was a satisfying, if Pyrrhic, victory for Mona, having won the battle but lost the war. She didn't get as much as she demanded, but she did get more than double what the government had offered.

The government, however, did not pay. July passed, and then August, and still no payment.

In September, lightning stuck. The government sought a new trial.

John W. McCulloch, an assistant U.S. Attorney for Bonneville affairs who had assisted Donaugh in the trial, filed an appeal alleging a mistake by Judge McNary. McCulloch argued that McNary improperly allowed several real estate experts who were called by the defense to speculate on the value of Mona's property if it were subdivided and sold as individual lots. McCulloch quoted from the testimony of several defense witnesses, including Amedee Smith, who replied when asked how he had arrived at his valuation of $110,000 to $125,000: "That tract of land can be laid off into approximately 100 town lots. Thirty six of those lots could be sold at an average of $1,000. Half the remainder could be sold at $500 each and the other half at $300 each." McCulloch had objected at the time, but McNary had overruled him.

Speculation about future value is not permissible in determining present value, McCulloch argued, citing case law in support. This was a reversible error, he argued.

In response, Bowerman introduced a motion to order the government to deposit an amount equal to the verdict in the first trial with the clerk of the court essentially as collateral—an account Mona could draw on, as her bills were mounting and she was without regular income—Bowerman did not mention interest payments from her son's trust fund. The government had allowed her to continue living in the house even though she had been ordered to vacate by July—now two months earlier—but she did not have enough cash or credit to move. Not only had the government not paid, but the construction work was continuing and her land was being destroyed, Bowerman wrote, reiterating a complaint he made in his original reply brief in March 1934, 18 months earlier.

Quoting from Bowerman's motion, *The Oregonian* reported that the government "has damaged the property in question by cutting and removing trees, by placing on the land piles of rocks, by destroying garden land, by erecting a school house, building portions of dwelling houses, and constructing barracks," adding, "the government now threatens to divert the water supply." Bowerman argued that all of this made clear that the government intended to take the property, and so it made sense for the government to make a deposit based on the result of the first trial while Mona awaited the second trial.

Judge McNary considered the motions and, on Nov. 5, denied Bowerman's motion, granted McCulloch's, and ordered a new trial to begin the following April.[44]

Mona left no record of the winter of 1934-35. There is no evidence that she moved from the Gorge. Presumably, she continued to live on her hilltop while the dam construction work continued apace below and all around her. It is not clear today whether she had another source of income than her son's monthly trust-fund checks.

There is no further newspaper coverage until April 1935, when *The Oregonian* reported on the beginning of the second trial and the encore performance of then ex-Governor Meier, who had left office in January when his four-year term expired.[45]

As with the first trial, a transcript could not be located, but the events and testimony can be reconstructed from newspaper coverage. This time the jurors included a real estate salesman, a janitor, a grocer, and the owner of a service station.

Once again, Meier placed the value of the estate at more than $100,000, which remained Mona's asking price. *The Oregonian* reported: "Ex-Governor Meier testified that he went over the property more than 20 years ago with the late Sam Hill, ex-owner, and that he had considered it at that time a beautifully rugged piece of land." Meier is quoted, "It is the most beautiful piece of property in that vicinity aside from my own." The government had not changed its offer from $26,500.

The trial continued for several days. On April 17, the *Journal* reported that George Playter, a real estate expert called to the stand by the government, testified that he agreed with the government's valuation of Mona's estate, but under cross-examination he said he also was familiar with comparable estates in the Tualatin River valley southwest of Portland that had sold for $100,000 to $125,000. Bowerman or his associates also forced a piece of damaging testimony from real estate expert John Lewis, who also had appraised the estate for the government. Lewis admitted that he had disclosed the government's offer of $25,600 to Henry E. Reed, another government witness, before Reed submitted his appraisal, at the request of the government, of $24,500.

The government witnesses testified that John G. Barnett's two leases with Mona, totaling about 2 1/3 acres, did not add value to the property even though they would generate $5,000 in income for Mona over the five-year lease periods. By the time of the second trial, Mona and Barnett had ended the leases, as the land clearly was going to be taken over by the government.

The trial ended, the jury deliberated and again found in favor of Mona. This time the award was $72,500—$2,500 less than at the first trial—and again with 6 percent interest from the date of the condemnation order in February 1934. The *Journal* reported on the verdict—on Page 1, only the second time either trial made the front page—and noted that there was a bit of victory for the government. In this second trial John Barnett was not a defendant, as the leases had been canceled, and this saved the government the $8,000 Barnett was awarded in the first trial. On the other hand, it meant that Barnett received nothing.

The verdict of the jury in the second trial was filed with the court on April 19, 1935, one day after the trial ended, and the final judgment was signed by Judge McNary on April 26. The order gave the government 30 days to submit a "bill of exceptions"—in essence, an appeal. On the 30th day, the government asked for another 30 days, but Judge McNary refused. The verdict stood, but the government still did not pay. An agonizing month passed, a month in which Mona could only look down from her hilltop on the continued destruction of her estate as construction crews built the massive dam and the instant town of Bonneville.

Then, in a letter dated May 31, 1935, Major C.F. Williams, District Engineer of the Second Portland District of the U.S. Army Engineer Office, told Mona to get out. In dry legalese that ignored the 15-month court saga just ended, Major Williams advised Mona that the federal government "was allowed to take immediate possession" of her home by order of the District Count of Feb. 9, 1934, and that the government officially took possession of the property on Feb. 10, 1934. The government "subsequently permitted you to occupy the dwelling on said land free of charge pending the time that particular portion of said tract should be needed in connection with the construction of the Bonneville Dam," the letter continued. Apparently that time had come, coincident with the end of the second trial and the jury's verdict. "Your permit of occupancy is hereby cancelled," the letter said, "and you are requested to vacate said premises on or before midnight, June 10, 1935."

Thus, Williams gave her 10 days to get out—11 counting the date of the letter—but the government still had not paid. And Mona was not about to move without payment. In fact, she couldn't afford to move.

On June 6, four days before she was supposed to be out, Mona's attorney Jay Bowerman filed an affidavit with Judge McNary, including a copy of the eviction notice, complaining not only that she had not been paid but also that the government, since February 1934, had caused extensive damage to the property.

The affidavit reminded the court that at the second trial the jury awarded Mona $72,500 plus interest at 6 percent from February 9, 1934, an amount that now totaled more than $78,000. Having taken possession of the property, the Army "... has cut large amounts of timber therefrom and destroyed large and valuable improvements thereon made by this defendant, and has erected buildings and parts of buildings on her said property, but has allowed her to reside in the dwelling house subject to eviction on short notice." The government improvements, listed in the affidavit, included railroad grades, a public schoolhouse, portions of two residences, an administration building and another building (probably this was the gymnasium/community center which, like the administration building, lay immediately below her home and, in fact, remains there to this day). If the government could afford to do all of that, the government surely could afford to pay Mona, Bowerman argued.

The affidavit also complained about the short notice Mona had been given. The letter from Major Williams, sent by registered mail, arrived at her home on the hilltop at 7:30 p.m. on June 4, even though it was dated May 31, giving her just six days to vacate. This was a problem, according to the affidavit, as "this defendant is without money. Her deposit account in her bank is overdrawn. . . .she has a large amount of valuable furniture in her home and has no place to take the same and is without even the means necessary to suitably crate and move and store said furniture." The expense of the two trials sapped her savings: "In carrying out this litigation this defendant has been compelled to rely almost exclusively on borrowed money, and her credit is now practically if not entirely exhausted, and for said reasons this defendant is not situated where she can comply with said order without great distress, damage and injury."

In short, the government had not filed a bill of exceptions, nor did Mona plan to appeal, but she could not move unless the government paid. Accompanying the affidavit was a motion ordering the government to pay the amount awarded by the jury as ordered by the court. This prompted the last newspaper coverage of the trials. An article in *The Oregonian* for June 25 reported in part: "The matter was before the court as a motion of Jay Bowerman, Mrs. Hill's attorney, who stated that Mrs. Hill has been ordered to be out of her home by noon yesterday and that soldiers would be there to put her into the street." The government's eviction notice did not mention soldiers or forcible eviction, but it was a nice touch, probably prompted by something Bowerman said in court or to the reporter who wrote the article. Sensibly, the article inferred, Bowerman asked the court to order the government to pay his client before evicting her.

Sensibly, it could be argued, the government did not file a reply, having lost the case twice and now being portrayed in *The Oregonian* as on the verge of sending soldiers to evict a woman and her six-year-old son from their home without paying her the money that had been awarded by two juries. Judge McNary signed Bowerman's order, and on July 10, 1935, the War Department delivered a check to the court in the amount of $78,661.50.[46] A check in that amount, made out to Mona, was delivered to Bowerman's office the next day.[47]

Interestingly, Mona's marital status never was a matter of interest to the press. While Bonneville residents seem to have understood that Mona and Sam had been lovers, newspaper stories about the trials only implied a relationship, and that more of a friendship. The stories didn't explore the obvious cooincidence that both Mona and Sam had the same last name. Mona signed her court documents E. Bell Hill. The *Journal*, *Oregonian*, and *Evening Telegram* newspapers always referred to her as the owner of the property and, by name, Mrs. E. Bell Hill on first reference and Mrs. Hill on subsequent references. Only one article of some two dozen that were published during the trials, a period of time encompassing February 1934 through June 1935, tied the two together, and then only to note that Sam selected the site of Mona's home and that she named her son after him. In court documents, Mona always was described as a widow. Newspaper accounts did not describe her marital status at all, noting only that she lived at her "country estate," as it was frequently described, with her son. There is no mention of Mona's marriage to Edgar Hill, Sam's cousin, and Edgar certainly was not dead in 1934. In fact, he lived until 1945. So in describing herself as a widow, she must have been referring either to an earlier marriage or hoping no one would discover her marriage—nominal or actual—to Edgar.

Having fulfilled the court order by paying the final judgment, the government wanted Mona to move quickly. However, the Army did not set a new deadline for her to leave, perhaps hoping to avoid another dose of soldiers-evicting-mother publicity. Or, perhaps a story Mona would tell her son many years later was true—that she planned to defend her home to the end with her own gun, and she let the Army know that. Perhaps, then, the government sensibly decided not to push the matter but instead wait for Mona to announce she was ready to leave.

There is no eye-witness account of the final skirmish between Mona and the Army. It took place eight days later on July 19, 1935, when Mona handed the keys to Captain J.S. Gorlinski, Resident Engineer at the Bonneville Project. For Mona, of course, it was a sad day and one she never would forget. In a curt memorandum on the transaction, Major Williams reported to his superior, the Chief Engineer of the Northwestern Division of the Army Engineers, that Mona had "... been granted a reasonable time to arrange for other quarters," and that Captain Gorlinski "found the premises to be in a satisfactory condition."

And so Mona left the place that had been her delight and refuge for 2,482 days—legally, from Oct. 2, 1928, when Sam Hill deeded the property to her, until the day she "vacated and delivered the premises," in the words of Major Williams' memo. She remained a woman alone, except for her son, now nearly seven years old. Her lover had been dead four years, she had a substantial sum in the bank, the responsibilities of motherhood did not suit her, and the old wanderlust was a Siren's song. She left the Columbia River Gorge and never returned.

Later in life, when Mona talked about the trials, it was always in anger.

"She hated what the government did to her," her daughter-in-law, Virginia Hill, said. "She thought they were crooks."

CHAPTER 7

Private Showplace to Public Derelict

*H*OUSING WAS ONE OF THE BIGGEST CHALLENGES AT THE BONNEVILLE PROJECT. WORKERS POURED INTO THE AREA AND OVERWHELMED THE AVAILABLE SUPPLY OF HOMES, APARTMENTS, AND ROOMS FOR rent. But the government undertook a crash construction project to accommodate the workers. By the end of January 1934, a month before Judge McNary signed the condemnation order for Mona's property, the government had constructed a camp for workers that consisted of six dormitories, a mess hall, hospital, office, and kitchen. It would grow over the next year and a half to include dozens of additional dormitories and work buildings. In the spring of 1934, there were 285 government employees at Bonneville; by January 1936, the number was 880.[48]

In the spring of 1934, foundations were laid for a planned residential community for the dam's permanent staff. These 20, two-story frame homes, completed the following November, were designed by Portland architect Hollis E. Johnston in a colonial revival style and laid out on curving, landscaped streets.[49] They were unique structures, built by carpenters who, short on nails, made extensive use of joinery. The flat land where the homes were built had been Mona's.

The War Department also moved quickly to remodel the mansion on the hill once Mona was evicted. Johnston prepared a plan for converting the house into two apartments, one on the main floor and the other on the upper floor. The plan is dated July 16, 1935, three days before Mona turned over the keys to Captain Gorlinski.

While the mansion had the capability of being something of a dormitory—Mona had rented rooms to itinerate workers in the past, including surveyors for the Bonneville Project—the Army decided to make just two large apartments. On the first floor, the living room remained a living room, but the same-sized master bedroom directly above became the new living room of the upstairs apartment. Both rooms had fireplaces. What had been a large walk-in closet off the old master bedroom became a den, and an enclosed alcove on the view side of the bedroom is labeled "new breakfast RM" on the plan. An adjacent room that had been a den, possibly, also on the view side, became the new kitchen for the upstairs apartment. On the main floor, two new bedrooms were added, and a room that may have been a bedroom facing the front of the house adjacent to the garage was converted to a laundry and "fuel room." The old laundry was remodeled into one of the new bedrooms. The existing front door and the steps to the second floor, which rose through the turret, were removed and replaced with new steps—four up to a landing and then six more to the second floor. A new wall to enclose the remodeled vestibule was built and two new doors were installed, one at the base of the new steps, creating separate entrances for the two apartments.

Mona long believed the Army wanted her house for the chief engineer of the project, or for some of the other executives. "She spent about three years and $40,000 fighting" the government, her son, Sam B. Hill, said in a 1985 interview. "The principal reason they wanted the place was because the chief engineer wanted the house on the hill for his residence, and that infuriated my mother."

That may or may not be true, and while Bonneville Project executives may have lived there during the later phases of the construction effort, they were not the first residents. That honor went to Fred and Fern McGhee, who were the first to live in the downstairs apartment, and Oliver and Frances Moreland, who were the first to live upstairs, according to Lorena Fisher, who lived at Bonneville from 1935 to 1942 while her husband, Larry, worked at the dam as an electrical engineer. In her memoir, *The Bonneville Dream*, Fisher writes that the Morelands invited friends to visit and there were frequent parties, but that "so far as I know, no one ever saw the lower-floor apartment" except for the McGhees.

In a 1985 interview, Lorena recalled her time at Bonneville as exciting and fun. She and her husband lived in the federal village at the base of the hill below Mona's mansion, which they recalled visiting.

"It was a very attractive place with nice landscaping" Lorena said. "There was a dressing room upstairs that had a whole bunch of mirrors.

These all made you look skinnier than you were. We women used to love to go up there when we went to the house for parties. You could see yourself on three sides."

She notes in her book that in October 1934, two Army officers—Resident Engineer Capt. J. Gorlinski and his chief administrative officer, Capt. Colby Meyers—were assigned to manage the construction project, and they lived in two houses in the federal housing at the base of the hill, not in Mona's mansion.

The advent of the instant community of several thousand people at Bonneville was the largest infusion of industry, technology, and people to the Columbia River Gorge to that time, but certainly not the first. The Gorge was the water route through the Cascade Mountains, a transportation corridor for Native Americans who had lived along the river for thousands of years, for Euro-American explorers who first arrived in the early 1800s, and later for fur trappers, miners, missionaries, and travelers on the Oregon Trail, many of whom made their last, sometimes perilous, push down the Gorge to the tidewater communities of Oregon City and later Portland. And then slowly over time, the tidewater communities grew and prospered, and the Columbia and the highways and railroads along its northern and southern shores through the Gorge became the water and land routes to and from the mining and agricultural areas east of the Cascade Mountains and the sawmill and fishing communities along the lower river, the estuary, and the ocean. The importance of the Columbia as the economic engine of the region steadily increased. It was inevitable the water and the power of the Columbia—it is the fourth-largest river by volume in North America—would be put to work making electricity and providing navigation for barges moving up and down the river.

The Columbia River Gorge of the mid-1930s rapidly was becoming something more industrial and less romantic and mysterious than the place Sam Hill opened with the Columbia River Highway, a road he promised to build so that "the world can come out and see the beauties of the land out of doors," in the Gorge, which he described as a place of "magnificence and grandeur." It was still grand and magnificent, but steadily it was being populated, exploited, and changed. Sam was well aware of the increasing traffic on the highway, and appears to have been proud of it, at least as it proved him right about the need for good roads to link growing cities and enable commerce. In 1928, he told historian Fred Lockley: "When the Columbia River Highway was being built and I prophesied that the time would come when, instead of having five- or seven-passenger cars, there would be regular stages and buses, carrying as many as 12 people at a time, to Seattle and to The Dalles and to other points in the state, I was jeered at and called a dreamer and visionary."[50]

Eight years later, in April 1936—Sam had been dead five years—the Oregon State Highway Engineer, R. H. Baldock, presented a plan to the state Highway Commission to straighten and widen the Columbia River Highway from Troutdale to The Dalles. The old highway was scenic, Baldock wrote in the plan, but the road was slow because of its many twists, turns, and elevation changes. Of course, that is precisely what Sam Hill and Sam Lancaster planned—a road like those in the Swiss Alps that follows the natural contours and makes travelers participants in the landscape, enhancing their appreciation of nature, rather than making them mere observers from a distance. The vision in the state's plan was much different: a water-level superhighway along the shore of the river that would speed travel between Portland and The Dalles, and also improve the safety of the road by skirting the cliffside tunnels—another Sam Hill and Sam Lancaster inspiration to highlight the natural splendor of the Gorge, but which the plan described as narrow and dangerous.

Straightening and widening the road would be good for business and also a benefit for tourists, who would enjoy the Gorge from a new vantage point. According to the plan:

> "The economic importance of this road should not be underestimated, as its construction will enable industries in Oregon to recapture markets in Eastern Oregon, Eastern Washington, and Idaho that have been taken by Seattle interests. … The water-level route will have a beauty in distinct contrast to the present road, affording an intimate view of the river and, being sufficiently far from the hill, will permit a view of the waterfalls even more advantageous than at present. There are

extensive sandbars adjacent to the river available for bathing beaches. ... The present Columbia River Highway between Troutdale and Dodson will remain undisturbed and be available as a park road, and from the high, rocky promontories the beauties of the Columbia River Gorge can be leisurely viewed without danger from the fast traffic. The old and new highways will make a delightful loop drive dislocating the varied beauties of the Columbia River Gorge as never before." [51]

The section between Troutdale and Cascade Locks, a distance of about 30 miles, was particularly troubling to the state highway engineers because of its ups, downs, curves and narrow profile. Just in that section alone, the flatter, straighter, faster road along the Columbia River shore would be about four miles shorter, eliminate 3,300 feet of elevation changes, and reduce the angle of curves, compared to the existing road, by 10,054 degrees, which the report compared to 20 times around a circle.[52]

The Oregonian, reporting on the plan for the new highway, quoted Baldock proclaiming that the savings in gasoline and vehicle maintenance would equal the cost of the construction in 15 years. The article continued: "The ordinary tourist and the motor freight lines who now toil up the grades and then wind down treacherous loops will be benefitted."

Construction of the new road to Cascade Locks would be accomplished in segments, and the first segment, just east of Mona's property, already was complete. In 1935, the year Mona was evicted, the Highway Commission and the Army cut a new path through a high ridge east of Eagle Creek for the highway and the Union Pacific Railroad tracks. By April 1936, a highway bridge was under construction over Eagle Creek, and the state's Bureau of Public Roads sought bids to build the 837-foot Tooth Rock tunnel.[53] The highway commission also planned to contract for completion of a 1.2-mile segment that would realign the road below Mona's hilltop.

Meanwhile, the State of Oregon hoped to acquire Mona's house as an addition to state park land near the dam. At some administrative level, the Army had decided that it no longer needed the house on the hill—this was less than a year after the house finally had been acquired, and remodeled at government expense. The District Engineer, Major C. F. Williams, the man who signed Mona's eviction notice, was holding up the transfer to the state. Apparently he wanted to keep the house, but others in the Second Portland District were ready to declare the property surplus to the Army's needs, and the state was willing to push the matter aggressively, if politely.

Surviving documents suggest that the key unresolved issue between the Army and the state, officially at least, was the alignment of the new highway interchange for Bonneville Dam. Work on the stretch of highway between Tooth Rock and Eagle Creek—past the house—could not begin until the state and the Army agreed on the location of the realigned highway and the Bonneville Dam interchange. In an April 12, 1937, letter to Baldock, J.M. Devers of the state Parks Commission wrote: "You will recall that representatives of the Army have several times assured us that it was the purpose of the government ultimately to deed to the State of Oregon such portions of the Hill property as the Government may not care to keep." Devers wrote that at the request of Parks Commission Director Samuel Boardman, he had asked the Army when it planned to turn over the property and that Major Williams had replied by letter, advising: ". . .final disposition . . .of the Hill property . . .is being held up in this office pending submission by the Highway Commission of a solution to the proposed new highway location in front of the entrance to the Bonneville grounds." Devers asks Baldock for a conference on "the Government's request with respect to the proposed highway location" and adds:

> *"I think it would be well if the State could get the Hill property before some new plan is worked out, for it may be that somebody employed in connection with the management of the dam or the distribution of energy may want that home to live in. I think we should speed up our arrangements if possible."* [54]

Boardman, a friend of Mona who had testified on her behalf at the condemnation trials, clearly wanted her house for the state parks department. Boardman saw the transfer as essentially compensation for 25 acres adjacent to Mona's property that the state donated for the dam in 1933.[55]

A year passed.

In April 1938 Devers again wrote to Baldock advising him that the state was still waiting for the property transfer and reminding him that the Army had responded to his last inquiry with a letter reiterating that the property would not be transferred until the matter of the entrance to the Bonneville grounds was resolved. Neither letter precisely describes the problem, but it is clear that Major Williams, the one who would approve the transfer, still was the one holding it up. But arm-twisting probably would not work with the stubborn Major Williams, Devers wrote:

> *"From this reply it is apparent . . .that if the State is to get the Hill residence it will be through some diplomatic arrangement with the Army. I am sure that if we attempt to go over their heads we will only embitter them and the Washington office will no doubt sustain the local Army representatives. I think we should discuss this subject and see if we can't outline a course that will accomplish what we want."* [56]

Then, a stroke of luck for the state: a change of command at the Portland District of the Army Engineers meant Major Williams was out. In September, Boardman wrote to Devers that with Williams gone it might be a good time to take up the matter with Don E. Meldrum, the senior land engineer with the Portland District of the Army Engineers, who always had been favorable to the transfer. If Meldrum was familiar to Boardman, he doesn't mention it. Meldrum was a witness for the government at the first condemnation trial, where he supported the government's low-ball offer.

Boardman wrote:

> *"I met a subordinate in his [Meldrum's] office some time ago on other business and incidentally mentioned this proposed donated Hill property to the State. He said that Mr. Meldrum had it in mind and was favorable to the transfer. (I believe it was Major Williams who objected to such a transfer. He is out of the*

picture now.) We graciously gave to the Government a park tract, at the dam site, containing twenty-five acres, the same costing the State park fund $7,500. I would appreciate it if you would drop Mr. Meldrum a letter of inquiry relating to this donation." [57]

Devers' letter to Meldrum is dated nine days later, September 24. It ends, courteously, "Can you tell me whether or not circumstances are such now that the transfer of the Hill property can be made to the State? Thanking you, I am, Yours very truly, J.M. Devers."

Six years passed.

Evidently, the circumstances were not such that the transfer could be made. Clearly, the Army continued to use the house or did not want to give it up.

If there was official correspondence between the state and the Army during those six years, it does not survive in the records of either the Oregon Department of Transportation (ODOT) or the real estate office of the Portland District of the Corps of Engineers.

On May 27, 1944, the patient J.M. Devers again wrote to Meldrum and this time received a reply from A.B. MacPherson, chief of the Division of Administrative Services of the Bonneville Power Administration. MacPherson wrote that Meldrum had transferred to San Francisco six months earlier and had been replaced by E. Wilbur Barnes. MacPherson suggested Devers contact Barnes and also write to Lt. Col. Ralph A. Tudor, district engineer in the Portland Office of the War Department. Devers did so on June 3. In that letter, Devers explains that Oregon's highway commissioners had asked him to report on the land transfer at their upcoming meeting in Portland on June 13. "I will thank you to let me know whether or not the Government has receded from the former plan and arrangement," Devers wrote.[58]

Apparently, the matter of the Bonneville Dam entrance alignment had been resolved, and so now, finally, there was some action. It took six more months, but on December 30, 1944, the real estate office of the War Department in Portland mailed the property deed to the highway commission in Salem, where it was received on January 2, 1945. A letter acknowledging the transfer was signed by E. Wilbur Barnes, who set the date of the title transfer as January 1, 1945.[59]

At the time, the house was being rented by a man named George E. McConnell. He had been renting the house from the War Department and now would be renting from the state. On January 22, Boardman wrote to Devers asking him to prepare a one-year lease dated January 1. The rent was $25 per month. The lease was renewed in January 1946. A Highway Commission memo refers to the house as "the residence building at Bonneville State park." McConnell may have been employed at Bonneville State Park, but no record of it remains today.

That same month, Boardman wrote to Devers that the new lease should stipulate that McConnell is required to maintain the residence and also "the landscaped grounds contingent to the residence" and the water supply reservoir and pipeline to the house. The state would buy any necessary parts for repairs, Boardman said.[60]

But the question of who was responsible for the water supply was not that simple.

Because the creek, cistern, and most of the pipeline that supplied water to the house were on federal land, the U.S. Forest Service had issued a special-use permit to the War Department to operate the water system in June 1936. Mona's state-issued water right dated to 1928, but when the government took possession of the property in July 1935 the private water right terminated. In a letter dated April 16, 1946, the U.S. Forest Service notified the state highway commission that because the War Department had transferred ownership of the house to the state, the state would have to apply to the Forest Service for its own special-use permit.[61] The state did so, and a permit was issued on April 22. Devers wrote a memo to the Highway Commission files dated three days later noting receipt of the permit and stating that it was his understanding that the permit gave the state the same water rights as the War Department had when it owned the property.

But it was not that simple, either.

The Forest Service copied its April 16 letter to the War Department, which responded with a letter to the Forest Service dated May 28. In that letter, the War Department said its special-use permit for the water supply was issued by the Forest Service in 1936 and that the water line ran across a piece of the property acquired from Mona Hill in 1935. That piece of property was conveyed to Multnomah County

School District 46 in July 1938. The Bonneville School was located on a piece of district-owned property—once Mona's and later conveyed by the federal government—immediately adjacent and was served by the same water line. The War Department assumed that the school had a permit to tap the line, and advised the Forest Service that the school and the state should share the new special-use permit with equal rights to the water.[62] Apparently that is what occurred for eight years, but in 1954 the water matter became an issue again. The cistern and pipeline, now 26 years old, needed repair.

Who would pay?

The school had closed, classes had been shifted elsewhere, and the school building had been sold to a private party. The Parks Commission found evidence that the school was using the water as early as 1936. In an interoffice memo, State Parks Superintendent (the parks department was part of the highway department at the time) C. H. Armstrong wrote: "It is presumed that some definite arrangement was made, probably with the Hills, before the land was obtained from the Corps of Engineers," according to the letter. But if Mona signed an agreement to share water with either the school district or the War Department, which built the school building as part of the new Bonneville community, there is no record of it today. In the letter, Superintendent Armstrong said the cistern at the head of the pipeline needed to be rebuilt, and that the cost would be several hundred dollars. He said the school district could be seen as having established a right to the water by using it for such a long period of time, a right that would have transferred to the new owner when the school building was sold. "Without proper arrangements we may find ourselves lacking in water for the facilities of the state park and footing a construction bill that will not be desirable," he wrote.[63]

In fact, the proper arrangements had been made, and Mona had an indirect, never-intended role. A Highway Department attorney researched the state's water rights archives and discovered that, in fact, Mona had two water rights—one issued in 1928 and the other in 1933. Both rights used the same pipeline. Together there was enough water from the two rights to serve the school and the house, but there were no written agreements allocating the water for purposes other than Mona's house and landscaping.

While there is no record today of Mona's intention for the second permit, Samuel Lancaster's Camp Get-A-Way had been destroyed by fire years earlier, and because Mona had leased portions of her property along the highway for commercial development, it is possible she planned another commercial development, such as a new campground. Or, because both water rights were allocated officially to her house, perhaps she simply intended to use more water—perhaps to expand her irrigation system for her hilltop landscaping.

At any rate, Devers, the Highway Department attorney, wrote in an interdepartmental memo dated January 6, 1955, that because the school district and the house used the same water pipeline, and because the original water right was sufficient for the present use of the house, "it is unnecessary to take any action at this time" against the current owners of the school building.[64]

The water dispute was resolved, but neither the house nor the school would stand for many more years, and the highway was continuing to change, as well. All were anachronisms in the present era. The school was old and small, and since the end of the dam construction era in the late 1930s there had been fewer and fewer students. The highway was still too twisty, too narrow, and occasionally too congested. And the house was just an old place on top of a hill.

Thus, by the mid-1950s, Sam Hill's vision of a winding, trail-like highway through the Columbia River Gorge, a route that would heighten the traveler's appreciation of the natural splendor of the only near-sea-level route through the Cascade Mountains, steadily was succumbing to the problems of its middle age. Ironically, it was this geographic fact of the Gorge that made it so desirable as a transportation artery—for high-speed commerce, not slow-speed tourism. All of the truck traffic, for example, between Portland and points east used the curvy, seldom flat highway—state Highway 14 on the Washington side was not much better—and as Baldock pointed out in his synopsis of the highway reconstruction plan back in 1937, the highway had to be straightened, widened, and flattened so that Portland would stop losing business opportunities east of the Cascades to Seattle. It might be the ultimate irony of the Columbia River Highway that the very commerce that Sam Hill envisioned as a principal reason for building it, connecting Portland to points east, now was the very thing that was making it increasingly obsolete.

That wasn't all.

The old road was becoming ever more dangerous. Rock slides and falling rocks were a constant problem. Three of the famous tunnels along the route, Oneonta, Mitchell Point, and the Mosier Twin Tunnels, had been abandoned and bypassed in the 1940s. All had been carved through solid rock and were among the iconic elements of the highway that made it so appealing to sightseers. Near the Mitchell Point Tunnel between Cascade Locks and Hood River, the rock slides were so dangerous and so constant that in the late 1930s—about 15 years earlier—the Union Pacific Railroad relocated its tracks away from the cliff and closer to the river. In the vicinity of each of the three tunnels, the highway pavement was scarred every few feet by the impact of falling rocks—some as large as three feet across. Maintenance was constant; vehicles had been damaged, and people had been injured. Sam would have been appalled that the highway he carefully crafted with Sam Lancaster, and which had been so carefully sited and almost lovingly built, now was causing injury, expense, and delay.[65]

Built at a time when autos were smaller and lighter and traffic volumes lower, the old road by the 1950s had become a continual source of frustration for the highway department. The state's reconstruction plan, which dated to about the time the Union Pacific relocated its tracks away from the bounding rocks near the Mitchell Point Tunnel, was nearing complete implementation—four lanes from Portland to The Dalles.

But the highway department did not abandon the old highway, at least in its most scenic parts. To this day, sections between Troutdale and Dodson, and between Mosier and The Dalles, remain open to traffic, as Baldock insisted they should. Writing in *The Oregonian* for Dec. 8, 1954, responding to a letter to the editor that claimed the department had "shabbily neglected" the old road, Baldock ticked off the safety problems related to falling rocks and landslides and stated: "It is believed that the highway commission has retained the most scenic portions of the old road except those sections which were positively dangerous adjacent to the tunnels." Other sections had been abandoned, he wrote, either over safety concerns or because there was no other possible route for the new road but in the same alignment as the old road. The highway below Mona's house was one of those places. "Between Dodson and Cascade Locks the new highway was built quite close to the old highway and in this operation much of the old highway was destroyed," Baldock wrote.

The Oregonian, on the same page, published an editorial supporting Baldock's conclusions. By preserving some of the old highway's unique and scenic route—past Crown Point, Multnomah Falls, the Rowena Loops, and so on—the highway commission "... is making a fair compromise between the practical and the aesthetic sides of the Columbia River highway question," according to the editorial. The "highway question" was how to preserve at least parts of the old highway for their scenic beauty while improving traffic flow and public safety through the Gorge. "We have Mr. Baldock's assurance that the graceful Italian stone railings that are so much a part of the charm of this route will be restored where they have crumbled away, and kept in good repair thereafter," the editorial advised. "That promise, along with the explanations given here today, should reassure those who want the old route kept in good repair so that future generations of motorists may enjoy its incomparable scenery."

But what of the incomparable house on the beautifully landscaped hilltop? The new, wider, realigned U.S. 30 clearly would replace the old meandering Columbia River Highway below the hill, and if anyone on the editorial page knew or cared about the fate of the structure, as unique in its way as the old highway, it was not evident.

Within five years the house would be demolished, but precisely when is a mystery. However, a general idea can be pieced together from two reports of the Oregon Parks Commission. Parks Commissioner Chester H. Armstrong reported in a parks history compiled in July 1965 that Bonneville State Park at that time consisted of 51.05 acres in five "fragmentary" parcels, as he called them, ranging in size from 3.76 acres to 25.36 acres. Armstrong wrote that the home "was occupied intermittently for several years" after the federal government deeded the property that included the hilltop and the home to the state.[66] In fact, by the mid-1950s the great brown, stuccoed, turreted home was abandoned, its windows boarded, and its once carefully manicured landscaping overgrown and neglected.

Armstrong continued: "At the time the Columbia River Highway was being rebuilt, in 1959, this home was sold.[67] It was demolished and removed from the area because a portion of the land was needed in the construction of the new highway. To provide access to the remaining area would have been very expensive, if not impossible. There has been no active public use of the area." [68]

Another, more romanticized, view of the fate of the house comes from Samuel Boardman, who, like his successor Armstrong, authored a history of the state parks. Boardman wrote:

> "Mr. [Sam] Hill bought a tract of land adjoining the [Bonneville State] Park on the south for his nephew, Walter Hill; wife, Mona Hill; [and] son, Sam Hill, living in Seattle at the time. He built a beautiful chateau on a high bluff overlooking the Columbia to the west. ... The U.S. Engineers needed a part of the property for the construction of the dam. The Hills refused to sell at the price offered by the government—$50,000. The Hills were asking $75,000. The case was taken to Court and a jury awarded the Hills the asking price of $75,000. This was too rich for the government and back to Court they went. This time a jury gave the Hills $82,000. The government rested its case, also licked its wounds."

Almost everything about this account is wrong, of course. Sam bought the property 11 years before he built the house, and he bought it for himself and Mona, possibly, as they may have been close at that time, not for any of his relatives; his cousin, Edgar, married Mona; her son was Sam's, not Edgar's; Sam had a brother-in-law named Walter (he was a son of James J. Hill), but no nephew named Walter; Mona and her son lived in the home by themselves; Edgar (Boardman's "Walter") never lived there; the government offered $25,600, not $50,000; the first trial ended with a jury award of $75,000, but that was not Mona's "asking price," which was $100,000; the government asked for a retrial over a procedural error, not necessarily because of the amount of the award although it is likely that was the motivation; and the second trial ended with a jury award of $72,500, not $82,000.

While Boardman can be faulted for his rendition of facts, his reminiscence otherwise is intriguing for his recollection of Mona herself. She was his friend. Boardman writes that at the time of his essay, which is dated March 12, 1952, "a park caretaker lives in the chateau on the hill where the Hills formerly lived." He does not identify the caretaker.

But then there is an odd transition in the narrative, or perhaps just a slip. Having consistently referred to "the Hills" living in the house, he suddenly refers only to Mona. Perhaps he knew the truth about her all along and chose to portray Mona as a married woman in his official history rather than as Sam Hill's mistress, alone on her hilltop with their little boy. Whether intentional or a slip, his observation is prescient:

> "Mrs. Hill and son Sam seemed to disappear from the earth when the government took over. Some eight years ago I received a card from Mrs. Hill. It was postmarked Shanghai, China. I have often wondered if young Sam would carry on in a capitalistic way." [69]

CHAPTER 8

Around the World

*T*HE CONDEMNATION BATTLE IN FEDERAL COURT IN PORTLAND DRAGGED ON FOR AN AGONIZING 15 MONTHS. WHEN MONA FINALLY LEFT OREGON IN JULY 1935, SHE TRAVELED QUICKLY, FIRST TO MINNESOTA, then to California and then out of the country. She was emotionally wounded, drained from the legal battle and ready for the tonic of travel. Journeying alone, taking risks, seeing new places, challenging the societal mores that confined women to supporting roles for the men in their lives—some women, at least—always had appealed to her. Once again, it was time to strike out on her own.

The substantial payment from the government was a compensation, and it would help pay for the freedom she craved, but it could not restore what she lost. She wanted to get as far away from Oregon, from the Army Engineers, from the memories, once sweet, now sad, as she could, and the sooner the better.

Mother and son traveled to Grand Forks, Minnesota, where Mona's mother, Esther, and sister, Frances, lived. Mona deposited Sam with them and left for California with plans to travel around the world.

She arrived in San Francisco, where she had lived some 20 years earlier, and attracted some attention. In a Sept. 6, 1935, article headlined, "Just Like a Woman," Edith Bristol, Women's Editor of *The San Francisco Call-Bulletin*, reported on the peripatetic Mona. The article, which affords Mona high-society status, begins: "If you have a palatial country home—and your Uncle Sam commandeers it for his needs—don't let homesickness get you down. Just take a world cruise, be gone a year and day, hunt big game in Africa, and be happy! That's the rule being followed by Mona Bell Hill as she starts out today on her globe-trotting expedition, sailing on the *President Coolidge* for a twelve-month voyage."

Evidently, Mona was not shy about talking about her mansion or how she lost it. Also evident is that by this time she and Edgar had divorced, or at least were no longer together in either fiction or fact, as the article describes her as "a former wife of a member of the famous Northwestern family." The article does not say whether Mona described herself as divorced or widowed—she had been described in press accounts of the trial in Portland as a widow, but Edgar would not die until 1945. Reporter Bristol wrote that Mona had been broken-hearted over the loss of her mansion but that she had decided, "travel is the best cure for homesickness."

At that point, she had been in San Francisco for three days, and just 50 had passed since she turned over the mansion to Captain Gorlinski.

Mona's mansion was "a magnificent place on the Columbia River" and for years was "one of the showplace homes of Oregon," according to the article, which continued: "Built by Samuel Hill, 'Empire Builder,' railroad tycoon and host to Queen Marie of Rumania, the imposing mansion was one of the best-known homes in Oregon." The home overlooked the site of Bonneville Dam, then under construction, the story reported, "and was included in the property set aside by the government in that giant undertaking."

Undoubtedly Mona had something to do with the hyperbola in the story. If the home truly were one of the best-known in Oregon and a show place, it had not been evident in newspaper coverage of the condemnation trials. The story made Page 1 only twice, both times in the *Oregon Daily Journal*, and both stories were less than three inches long. Even Governor Meier's testimony didn't rate Page-1 treatment in any of the three newspapers that covered the trial, *The Oregonian*, *Journal* and *Evening Telegram*. In all, the three newspapers published a total of 20 stories during the two trials, and none included a photo of the home, or of Mona, or of anyone connected with the condemnation proceeding, and none described the home as well-known or a show place. That the home was eye-catching and magnificently situated is indisputable, but its condemnation does not seem to have attracted more than modest attention in the press.

Mona also must have talked about her prowess with a gun, as the article reports that in addition to arranging visas and shopping for her trip, Mona was "making ready her camera for her preferred method of shooting big game in the African veldt. 'I can shoot with a gun,' she said, 'but the camera's better.'" [70] In fact, she would shoot with more than a camera in Africa. She gave her sister, Frances, the skin of a cheetah she shot—or claimed to. Frances hung the skin in the recreation room of her home in East Grand Forks, where it stayed for years, Frances' daughter, Bonnie Evans, said.

In 1935, the *President Coolidge* was the newest and, with its twin. the *President Hoover*, the largest of the passenger liners in the Dollar Steamship Lines fleet. Launched in Virginia in 1931, the ships were 654 feet long (615 feet at the water line). They catered to a well-heeled clientele. There were only two classes of tickets, first and second. In its advertising, the Dollar Lines promoted the sumptuous appointments, large guest rooms, fine food, and variety of entertainment on board. Appropriately, the Dollar Lines ships featured the company logo—a giant white dollar sign on a red background—prominently on the smokestack.

Despite the implication of the Sept. 6 article in the *Call-Bulletin* that Mona was departing that day, the ship left San Francisco on November 1, according to records in the San Francisco Maritime Museum. From San Francisco it was five days to Honolulu and nine more to Yokohama. From there, ports of call included, in order: Kobe, Shanghai, Hong Kong, Manila; Singapore, Penang, Colombo, Bombay, Suez, Port Said, Alexandria, Naples, Genoa, and finally Marseilles. Mona didn't leave a copy of her itinerary with her family, and so it is not known how long she stayed at any of these ports. The cost of a first-class ticket for the world tour was $745 (about $11,562 in 2008 dollars). A second-class ticket cost $625 ($9,700 in 2008).

She loved to tell stories about that trip, her son recalled.

"She went into the (Kenyan) bush without a white hunter, which was illegal," her son, Sam, said in a 1985 interview. "She was arrested in Kenya, but they didn't know what to do with her because she was a woman. So they let her go. Then she went to Uganda and did the same thing. She was an early day feminist for sure."

In northeastern Kenya, she traded her bloomers for a beaded leather apron being worn by a native woman. The two women communicated through sign language, and because of Mona's modesty, the trade was effected behind a large rock.

Mona had a movie camera and took several reels of film, but unfortunately the film cannot be located today. The apron, however, is preserved in a shadow box and hangs on a wall in Virginia Hill's home in the Los Angeles area. The woman who traded the apron "was so happy to see Mona Bell put it on, and she put on Mona's bloomers," Virginia said. "Really, she wanted Mona's bloomers more than Mona wanted her apron. She paraded around in them and was so pleased."

The provenance of the apron is something of a mystery. Two experts on East African body ornament reviewed photos of the apron and found it an interesting puzzle. One, Donna Pido, lives in Nairobi where she teaches and consults on sexually transmitted diseases. Her Ph.D. thesis in anthropology is in Maasai ornament.

"The beads on this piece look like they are recycled Turkana beads but I'd have to see a close up to be sure," she wrote. "The cut is basically Turkana but not quite. Turkana women and girls wear an under apron that ties around the waist and tapers to a narrow curve at the bottom. They usually use ostrich eggshell for the trim of under aprons. If the piece is Turkana, it can't be an outer apron—wrong shape. This piece is cut basically the Turkana way but without the curve that would fit below the waist in front. Also, the taper—which is probably the animal's tail-- is too pointed for Turkana. The beading technique and colors are consistent with Turkana style but the zigzag across the red, white and black fields is not. The trimming strands of what looks like 8/0 white rocailles is not Turkana at all. The Akamba sometimes trim items that way but they don't use the larger beads and do not sew borders that way."

She concluded one of her e-mails: "tis a puzzlement!"

The other expert, Bilinda Straight, is an associate professor of anthropology at Western Michigan University in Kalamazoo.

"It is hard to tell from the photo, but those slits have me wondering whether it is an upper body garment (a full garment could have three pieces—so the thing is to identify which piece this is)," she wrote after viewing the photos. "I work with Samburu in northern Kenya for example, and this is not at all like the skirts women in the lowlands wear (those who still wear them—fewer and fewer girls and women do) but the skirts they wear now are a bit different from what they wore, say, in the 1920s."

So it might be Turkana or it might be Akamba, and it probably is not Samburu, but whatever it is, Virginia is pleased to have it as a memento of her well-traveled mother-in-law. Like the apron, which might not be an apron, Mona was a mystery, and she would have enjoyed watching others try to figure her out. The apron proves she was in Africa, at least, but it sends mixed messages about where she might have been. That, it appears, will continue to be a mystery.

One letter survives to give a flavor of Mona's global escapade. It is addressed to her sister, Frances, and written on stationery of the Shepheard's Hotel, Cairo. Mona crossed out Cairo and wrote in "Beirut, Lebanon," and the envelope is sealed with three gold, circular stickers embossed with the name of the historic St. George's Hotel. The postage stamps are Lebanese; the postmark is blurred but appears to be in late March 1936. It arrived in East Grand Forks on April 17.

In the two-page letter, Mona is chatty about her travels in a way that must have stirred envy back in rural Minnesota. "Frances, dear," Mona writes, "Enclosed please find the bill to be presented to customs when goods arrive. There is a 40% duty on rugs—15% on brass, so I am told. I have been quite extravagant in brasses, but I couldn't get them in India and other countries because I could not carry them. ... Let me know when you hear from goods shipped from Manilla." Mona had been ill with a bad cold for three days, she wrote, but, "they gave me two perscriptions [sic], a short wave light treatment on chest and a infra-red light treatment on head and it worked like magic (There is an American university in this town.)"

And she asked about Sam: "How is my darling boy—Tell him his mumsie loves him heaps. Will enclose some more stamps for him in this letter. Hope he's taking good care of them. Sometimes someone gives me old and rare stamps." She ended with three cities where she would be able to receive mail via American Express in the coming two months—Athens, Rome, and Paris. She signed the letter a bit formally for a sister, "Mona Bell Hill."

CHAPTER 9

The Savvy Investor

*W*HEN MONA RETURNED FROM HER WORLD TOUR, SHE HAD INCOME AND DID NOT HAVE TO WORK TO EARN MONEY, THANKS TO THE GOVERNMENT'S PAYMENT FOR HER COLUMBIA RIVER GORGE MANSION. She had invested the money in stocks, and later in her life she enjoyed bragging about how well she did over time, ultimately claiming to have quadrupled the initial amount.

She also had the income from the trust fund Sam Hill established for the benefit of their son. But this was a constant source of frustration, as the money was invested by bankers—the trustees—without her influence. Sam established the trust on Dec. 15, 1928, four months after baby Sam was born and two months after giving Mona the hilltop property in the Gorge. The $60,000 principal was in bonds issued by Sam's investment firm, the United States Trust Company, and paid 5 percent interest. Sixty thousand dollars was a lot of money in 1928. Assuming an average annual inflation rate of 3.18 percent, $60,000 in 1928 would have the buying-power equivalent of $732,000 in 2008.

The bonds matured on May 15, 1936. In the wake of Sam's death in 1931 and the legal battle over the probate of his will, Seattle-First National Bank had taken over as administrator of the trust. In fact, the bank managed all three trusts for Sam's children by his mistresses. In each case, the principal amount was $60,000, the principal was to remain intact, interest would be paid to the mothers as guardians of their children, and when the children died, the principal amounts would be paid to Maryhill Museum, not to the mothers.

While Sam's trust referred to Mona as his guardian, no formal declaration of guardianship had been established. From 1928, when the trust was established, until his death in 1931, Sam Hill simply sent checks in the amount of the interest made out to Mona—not to young Sam with Mona as guardian.[71] After he died, the United States

Trust Company continued the practice, and when the bonds matured, Mona assumed Seattle-First would do the same. In correspondence and legal documents, she was variously described as the guardian of her son, the trustee of his trust, and the income beneficiary.

However, the maturation of the bonds posed a dilemma for the bank: how to reinvest the principal amounts of the three trusts. In declaring the trust, Sam Hill left no instructions regarding reinvestment. Perhaps he intended to outlive the eight-year life of the bonds. But he did not.

So the bank's attorneys asked Mona, as a trustee, how she would like the money reinvested and then filed a friendly lawsuit in King County Superior Court to obtain a judge's approval for amending the trust language. The original principal amount was solely in United States Trust Company bonds, and the bank considered their 5-percent interest rate risky for the time. Too risky, the bank's attorneys suggested: "In the present condition of the security market it is not possible to reinvest said sum to produce such an income with safety," according to the bank's complaint.[72] They preferred a mix of long-term and short-term bonds issued by multiple companies, rather than a single large, and more risky, investment in a single issue.

Diversity and interest were less important to Mona, however, than the matter of her role and authority. She insisted that the revised trust should stipulate that she was the trustee for young Sam. She objected to the establishment of a formal guardianship. Mona apparently preferred the arrangement Sam Hill had established and wished to continue her control of the investments without more court involvement.

The bank filed its lawsuit against Mona and young Sam, as the immediate beneficiaries, and Maryhill Museum as the ultimate beneficiary of the principal amount after Sam and Mona were dead. All three trusts were restated at the same time through this proceeding with the court's approval.

The initial complaint was filed in King County Superior Court in Seattle on May 28, 1936, and final decrees were entered the following October. Part of the reason for the delay was that Mona was in Europe completing her world tour at the time the complaint was filed. Her letter to Frances includes her itinerary, apparently separate from some of the scheduled ports of call of the *President Coolidge,* as "Athens, April 15; Rome, April 30; Paris, May 15." It isn't clear when she arrived back in the United States, but she finally was served with the legal documents in early October. Bank attorney John Garvin states in his letter to Maryhill attorney Zola Brooks, dated October 6, that "service has just been made." [73] So Mona either was served in France or elsewhere in Europe, or she was back in the United States by then, having left the ship before its final destination. The letter does not say where she was served the papers.

The matter finally was completed in January 1937—but not without more arguing by Mona. "During the past two weeks Judge W.D. Askren and myself [sic] have been endeavoring to satisfy Mrs. Hill as to the provisions of the reinvestment decree," Garvin wrote to Brooks on December 3, 1936. Mona wanted the decree to stipulate that the principal could be invested only in bonds with a Moody's rating of AA or higher, and the bank's investment officers thought A-rated bonds should be included, as well, because "many state bonds which are perfectly good although regarding which there is not much turnover . . . are oftimes [sic] desirable investments." [74] The bank prevailed on this point, and the final decree was dated in January 1937. According to the decree, the principal amount was to be invested ". . . in mortgages or in bonds rating 'A,' 'AA,' or 'AAA' with a view in the judgment of the trustee of securing the best possible return consistent with sound investment practices." [75]

But Mona prevailed on the question of her authority. The decree stipulated that the bank would pay Mona, as trustee for her son, the net income after expenses, insurance, and commissions "during the term of his natural life, and in the event of his death prior to her death, pay such income to her during the term of her natural life." The court also interpreted the terms of the trust to mean that it would not terminate until they both died, and that the one who survived the other would continue to receive the payments until his or her death, at which time the entire principal amount would transfer to Maryhill Museum.

Mona remained anxious about the bank's investment strategy. For decades afterward she monitored the progress of the trust fund carefully.   Periodically, she complained to Seattle-First National Bank that a more aggressive portfolio would make her more money. In July 1946, for example, possibly at Mona's instigation, Maryhill attorney Zola Brooks met with an attorney for the bank to discuss the status of all three trusts, which at that point had declined in value.   The principal amount of young Sam's trust had dipped to $56,154, and the other two had declined farther. In September of that year, Mona apparently met personally with Brooks, as the Maryhill archives include a letter of introduction from the attorney who represented her in the condemnation proceedings, Jay Bowerman of Portland. Bowerman was cryptic in his explanation of the reason for the requested meeting, writing only that she "desired to acquaint you with some facts concerning matters of interest to her which she feels should be of interest to you, relative to some of the Samuel Hill matters." Bowerman added a personal recommendation: "I have found Mrs. Hill a responsible and dependable person in connection with all of the business I have had with her." [76]

If that meeting was in regard to the trust—it would not have been out of character for Mona to tell Brooks that Maryhill, the ultimate beneficiary of the trusts, was losing money—it may have done some good. Over the next 12 years, the trusts gained value. A page of notes on file in the Maryhill archives shows that in May 1958, the value of young Sam's trust was $61,910.25. The other trusts had gained value beyond the original amounts, as well. But the principal amounts still were invested in bonds, per the 1937 court decree, and after another 10 years passed Mona finally succeeded in convincing the bank to reconsider its investment decisions, as the value of the bonds had declined. She argued for more stocks and fewer bonds. This, however, would require either a court order or at least the approval of the Maryhill Museum trustees, and the bank was reluctant. In a January 1968 letter to Maryhill trustees, a Seattle-First National trust officer wrote that because of the bonds-only investment strategy mandated in the January 1937 restatement of the trust:

> ". . . the income beneficiary, Mrs. E. Bell Hill, has been receiving a limited income, and there has been minimal

appreciation in asset value for the trust. Mrs. Hill needs additional income, and she has repeatedly asked for more money from this trust.

"We could achieve a better combination of growth and income for the trust if we were to be allowed to invest in corporate stocks under the Prudent Man Rule. However, this would mean that we would have to petition the court to modify the investment provisions of the trust. And, of course, such court action would require the approval of the Maryhill Museum. Since the bonds held in trust have a face value of $61,000 and a market value of approximately $50,000, the trust asset value would be greatly reduced if we were to sell the bonds to buy corporate stocks." [77]

The trust officer said he hoped that if the bonds were sold to buy stocks, the loss would be made up over time through market value appreciation of the stocks, but there was no guarantee. "In essence," he wrote, "it would mean that the museum would be sacrificing some of its assets to provide a higher income for the income beneficiary." The officer asked for the trustees' advice. Museum Treasurer J.G. Scripps replied on January 25 that in his opinion the present time was not a good one to move from bonds to stocks, but that if the petitioner—Mona—allowed the bank latitude in the timing of the shift to take advantage of favorable conditions in the stocks and bonds market, the trustees would not object.

Mona was happy to oblige. While she had no formal training in investing, Mona had a strong interest in her own finances, and her investment success combined with her frugal lifestyle gave her the freedom to travel frequently while not being tied down to a regular job. Over time she became, if not wealthy, at least financially secure through her investments. She did this in a typically aggressive fashion, originally by investing some of the proceeds of the condemnation judgment in stocks when the stock market crash of 1929 still was a vivid memory and the nation was just pulling out of the Depression. In seven years she quadrupled her money, she would tell her son later in her life.

Thanks also to the trust fund payments from Sam, she had money, and she invested it. It's not hard to imagine that Sam offered her advice, although there is no record of it today, and given her spunk, it's also not hard to imagine her giving more weight to her own intuition than to Sam's advice.

"She liked AT&T," her daughter-in-law, Virginia Hill, said, recalling one of Mona's favorite stocks. Ironically, it was Pacific Telephone and Telegraph, later part of AT&T, that ran Sam Hill's Home Telephone Company out of business in Portland back in 1919.

CHAPTER 10

A Most Unusual Neighbor

*W*HEN MONA RETURNED TO MINNESOTA FROM HER PERIPATETIC WORLD TOUR, SOMETIME IN THE LATE SPRING OR SUMMER OF 1936, NOT ONLY DID SHE HAVE INCOME, SHE HAD A HOME, DESPITE HAVING LOST her mansion in the Columbia River Gorge. That is because in late September 1935, about a month before the *President Coolidge* sailed from San Francisco, Mona's mother, Esther, gave her a cabin and 74 acres on Dunbar Lake in north central Minnesota that she and Mona's father, Henry, bought in November 1926, about a year and a half before Henry died. From 1936 until 1953, Mona split her time between an apartment in Minneapolis, traveling, and the cabin on the lake.[78] The nearest community was unincorporated Squaw Lake, a small place then and still a small place—population 99 according to a modern-day sign on the edge of town along State Route 46, the Avenue of the Pines Scenic Byway.

Her home on the lake was an old hunting lodge. Her son lived with her when he wasn't at boarding schools. Mona hunted each fall, usually killed a deer, and when she did she would can the meat for later use. Most winters she moved to an apartment in Minneapolis, but she spent several winters at the snowy, frozen lake. When the hunting lodge was destroyed by fire in the late 1930s, she moved into a caretaker's shack on the property and then built her own cabin, smaller than the original, but quite comfortable. She also continued traveling, making many trips to Mexico, and always alone.

At her lake property, as she had at her hilltop mansion in the Columbia River Gorge, Mona planted a large garden—mostly flowers— where she perfected her mastery of lilies. She lived frugally, for the most part, but also enjoyed entertaining friends, some of whom she had met through Sam. One of these was Alma Spreckels of San Francisco, wife of Adolph Spreckels, heir to the family sugar fortune, who had been a close friend of Sam and who also had visited Mona's mansion in the Gorge.

Flowers were Mona's passion. Gardening was the thing she probably enjoyed most in life, aside from travel. Virginia Hill remembers that when her mother-in-law talked about her mansion in the Columbia River Gorge, she spoke first and most passionately about the landscaping and her garden.

"That was her love, really her love," Virginia said. "It was incredible to see her with her flowers."

Mona's love of flowers and gardening came from her mother. Lilies were Mona's favorite. She was a member of an international association of lily growers, and a cultivar, *Mona*, may be named for her. There was a secret to her prowess, Virginia said:

"She boiled her dirt. She said it helped improve the soil, but it was strange to see her boiling dirt. People would really laugh about how eccentric she was. You know, the old people up there in Squaw Lake really laughed about her boiling dirt."

But it worked. Mona grew award-winning lilies.

In fact, her garden covered more than an acre and she grew a variety of non-native flowers.

"Wonderful, luxurious flowers, types that were not from this area," said Dean Rajala of nearby Deer River, Minnesota. "She was well known for miles and miles for her flowers; in fact, I would say she was preeminent in our entire county for her exotic flowers."

Rajala was nine years old when he met Mona, in 1945.

"I was her summertime help," he said.

Rajala's grandfather, John Ronning, was Mona's nearest neighbor. She hired Ronning from time to time for a variety of jobs, including cutting and hauling firewood, and also helping her haul and distribute large loads of compost for her garden. Ronning's home and Mona's lakeside cabin were about a quarter-mile apart through woods.

"He adored her," Rajala said. "I think he was her closest friend in Minnesota."

Mona usually left the lake in the fall and returned in the spring, and Ronning would watch the place while she was gone.

"She was a most unusual woman," Rajala said. "She was frugal, very frugal. Her cabin was small and quite narrow, but beautifully located, just a beautiful place. I worked for her, and so did my sister, for just pennies an hour, you know. She paid my grandfather about 40 cents an hour—not a lot, but oh, did he work hard for her."

For Rajala and his sister, Doris, there were always little summertime jobs to be done around the cabin, the gardens, and the dock on the lake.

"She was very fussy about details, particularly about her flowers; she was a good employer in that regard," Rajala said. "She was very hands-on with me about what she had me do. She watched us very carefully. She would say things like, "you stepped on the flowers, Doris; your brother is more careful.""

Despite her frugality, she also had at least one trapping of wealth—a very nice car.

"Oh, it was a beauty, a big car, a Cadillac or a Chrysler. When she went into Blackduck to shop, she went in style," he said.

Rajala also knew Sam, who was eight years older.

"He was away a lot, but I did know him. I remember him swimming in the lake. He was a startlingly attractive boy and very nice, a kind of role model for me," he said.

The fact that Mona had a son but no evident husband was a curiosity, but she was apparently not the subject of vicious gossip the way she had been when she lived at Bonneville. Dunbar Lake is remote; neighbors looked out for and respected each other.

"We suspected she had a boyfriend, but we didn't know for sure," Rajala said. "All we knew about her past was that she was a relative of James J. Hill. We really didn't know her story."

The probable connection to James J. Hill also was what David Adams knew about Mona's background. Adams' parents bought Mona's Dunbar Lake property in 1972 from the family to whom she had sold it, and David and his wife, Marilyn, acquired it in 1996. They live in the Minneapolis area.

"There was a mystery about her," Marilyn Adams said. "We had no idea about her past life; we just heard she was somehow related to James J. Hill."

Everyone in northern Minnesota knew who James J. Hill was—a name probably as familiar as another famous immigrant to the state, George Weyerhaeuser. A family connection to The Empire

Builder would explain why Mona seemed well to do without having a regular job.

"She obviously was the wealthiest person in the area," David Adams said.

He recalled that after the original structure burned to the ground, Mona soon built her own home—the narrow, beautifully situated cabin that Rajala remembers. It was an unusual home, made up of eight separate rooms in four small attached structures. Some sections were built on site, and others were small structures that Mona moved to the property and added to what she had built. A neighbor, Harold Korpala, helped move a small building across the frozen lake one winter with a team of horses. The building became part of the rambling cabin.

"It was a nice little place, unusual for the era because it had two bathrooms—one with a shower and the other with a claw-foot bathtub, and she had electricity, which was very unusual for that area at that time; this was way back in the woods," Adams said. He speculated she either had a generator or somehow talked the local power company into running a line to her home from the main road, which was three-quarters of a mile away.

When Adams' parents bought the property, Mona's old cabin still stood but had not been used as a dwelling for a long time. It was a unique structure, not only because it was four attached buildings but also for its beautiful front door, brass fixtures, paned windows, and crystal door knobs. While nothing like the grandeur of her Bonneville estate, her Minnesota estate nonetheless was a showplace in its own right, with her trademark extensive, exotic landscaping. Adams, like Rajala, remembers Mona's remarkable flowers.

"She brought plants from all over the world and got them to grow in Minnesota," he said, impressed. Some of the poppies and day lilies Mona planted continue to thrive on the property.[79] Other mementos of Mona's time at the lake also remain. Some of her garden tools have been passed down through the owners of the property, and once when David Adams was digging near the roots of a large balsam tree, he uncovered broken pottery bowls painted with Chinese characters, most likely discarded by Mona.

Another who knew her was a neighbor farmer, Harry M. Miller, who worked in Mona's gardens in the 1940s, and possibly also in the

1930s, to earn extra money. One of his tasks was to prepare the gardens for Mona's return from her winter travels. His wife once snooped in Mona's bedroom while she was away and was surprised to find beautiful lingerie in her dresser drawers. It was a story she enjoyed telling friends and neighbors years after Mona moved away.

To her neighbors, Mona was something of a mystery woman. Irene Johnson ran a small store on the county road about two miles from Mona's cabin. Mona was a frequent customer.

"I never worked for her or that sort of thing," Irene said. "I was a country storekeeper. She would come in late in the afternoon for something to eat—a piece of meat, say. She wasn't too fussy about beef. We usually had just utility beef, anyway. She would ask me to trim it up, cut it real fine, and she would make minute steak from it."

While not fussy about her steak, she definitely could be about other things, Irene said. Her car, for one thing. While Dean Rajala recalls Mona driving a big, expensive car, that might have been later because Irene Johnson recalled a different one.

"She drove an older Ford. The roads were real bad. She was fussy about that car, though; she took care of it. I remember helping her change the oil." [80]

Mona didn't have a lot of friends in the area, but at the same time, she was not considered aloof or rude. Just alone, and something of a curiosity.

"We all knew she wasn't married," Irene said. "She did not have a lot of friends; she was not easy to get to know. She never did talk much about herself, and we didn't ask questions. We respected her. We didn't know anything about her personal history."

She was mysterious, an anomaly among the close-knit, sparsely populated rural community around the lake and the tiny outpost towns linked by rough country roads. There were rumors and assumptions—about her lavish lingerie, expensive jewelry, and her many rings, for example, and whether or not she had a boyfriend or ever had been married.

"She was financially well-off enough that she didn't have to get to know us country folks," Irene said. "But she appreciated what you did for her, that's for sure. That's how she was—not difficult to get along with, but she made clear what she wanted and she got what she asked for. She didn't socialize very much, but she wasn't standoffish, either. She would come to some of the social functions, like a wedding party for one of the locals, and maybe she'd bring a little present, but she didn't mingle that much. She was a different class, you know."

She also had a reputation for being handy with a gun, Irene recalled.

"My dad worked for her every once in a while. He was a jack of all trades. She shot a raccoon once and asked him to skin it for her. Well, the next day she had cooked it, and she offered him a piece of it. He thought, 'I'm not eating that.' So he told her he'd just had lunch. He'd never been that hard up that he had to eat a coon. Why she did, I don't know; maybe she was curious." Or maybe, as Mona's niece, Bonnie Evans recalled about her aunt, "Mona took great pride in her ability to eat anything. It was almost a point of honor with her that you try everything that's edible, be it coon, fish heads, or bugs."

Another neighbor, Art Schimanski, told David Adams how Mona let everyone in the area know, not long after she moved permanently to the lake, that she could take care of herself.

"Art told me that he went to see Mona one time, and she came out to meet him," Adams said. "They talked for a few minutes, and then Mona said, 'stay right here, I want to show you something.' Art said she went into the cabin and came out wearing a gun belt with two six-shooters. She then turned and shot the clothes pins off her clothesline at a distance of about 25 yards, firing one gun after the other—left, right, left, right. Art said it was like, bang-bang-bang-bang in rapid succession. He said he was aghast. Then she said to Art, 'you tell the boys there's a woman back here who knows how to shoot, and will shoot.' He did."

Another former neighbor who remembered Mona was Hugo Ojanen. In fact, while he was close in age to Sam, he knew Mona better because Sam was gone to school most of the year. Mona visited Hugo's parents from time to time. Her mailbox was at an intersection about halfway between the two homes, a place called Ronning's Corner after John Ronning, the adjacent landowner. Occasionally, Mona would employ Ojanen for little jobs around her house, usually in the garden. She also would give him letters to mail, and he noticed that many of them were addressed to investment companies.

"We knew she didn't work, and we assumed she lived off of her investments," Ojanen said. "She definitely did not have any boyfriends. She kept to herself, for the most part."

But not always.

He remembers seeing the movies she shot in Africa during her first around-the-world trip. There was a store in Squaw Lake called Kananen's, after the family that owned it. On the second floor was a dance hall. That's where she showed the movies to an audience of local people.

"I was about 10," Ojanen recalled. "I don't remember a lot of it, but I do remember a scene of natives in Africa, and the caption she wrote for the scene was 'comparing redheads.' I don't know what she meant by that—maybe she had red hair and they had dyed their hair red, and she was comparing herself to them."

Certainly, she was the only Squaw Lake resident who had gone on safari in Africa, and that only added to her mystique.

"She was kind of odd, you know," Ojanen said. "She was a recluse, for one thing. She had a telephone, but it wasn't in her house. It was in the garage, and the garage was 200 or 300 feet away from the house. She didn't use the phone to receive calls; she only called out. And she dressed differently than other women. To look at her, you'd think she was poor. She wore old snow pants or bib overalls, and she did not like to pay high wages. She did have a beautiful garden, and she was very particular about it. I remember that when she would have a load of manure delivered, she didn't think anything of digging the quackgrass roots out by hand."

Her interactions with neighbors included occasional sessions that only could be called physical therapy.

"Her leg would go out of place every now and then, and she would come over to have her leg pulled," Ojanen said. "I can't remember which leg it was, but I remember Jack Leinonen (another neighbor) saying, "I don't like those leg-pulling parties very much.""

What he and the other neighbors knew about Mona was that she lived humbly, traveled extensively—sometimes she bought Ojanen's father a bottle of rum when she visited the Caribbean—and otherwise kept her past to herself.

He was surprised to learn about Mona's relationship with Sam Hill, and young Sam's parentage.

"That woman had a heck of a past that we didn't know anything about," he said.

If her Dunbar Lake friends and neighbors thought she was related to James J. Hill, she apparently did not correct the assumption. Later, if people suspected she was somehow related to Sam Hill, as she had been described during the Bonneville litigation in Portland, that was OK, too. She kept a large, framed portrait of Sam in her home and was pleased to show it to visitors. To anyone who asked, Sam was a relative.

Their love affair was her secret.

"She never talked about any of that," Virginia Hill said.

Direct, argumentive, assertive—these were the keystones of Mona's prickly personality. And yet, just as quickly she could be loving and kind. That is how Virginia Hill recalls Mona, dating all the way to her first encounter with her future mother-in-law in the early 1950s.

"Mona Bell—I always called her by both names—was in East Grand Forks at the time, and Sam and I went to see her. After we were introduced, she said, 'I'd like to speak with you in the bedroom.' So we went in there alone, and she said, 'why do you want to marry my son? You know, he has many problems.' This is how direct she could be. So I said I was aware of his problems but that we were in love and wanted to marry. We went back and forth for awhile, and then she said, 'I would love for you to marry my son.' And that was that."

Virginia said Mona then opened a box of silver jewelry she had purchased in Mexico—she loved jewelry—and said, "pick out the one you like the best, and it's yours." Virginia did, a necklace. Later, she inherited the entire box.

Mona could be, in one moment, direct to the point of confrontation, and in the next moment, generous to the point of lavishness. It was a personality trait that others noticed, from casual acquaintances to her closest relatives.

Virginia recalled that once she and several friends met Mona at her cabin at Dunbar Lake. "I warned my friends before we went that my mother-in-law could be difficult to deal with, and my friends all said, 'oh, we'll be fine.' Well, we weren't there half an hour before one of my friends came running into the kitchen crying, literally in tears. She said, 'that woman is terrible!'"

Mona was a competent cook, but frugal about it, as was her personal style, her daughter-in-law said.

"She loved good food and constantly gave me compliments. She loved simple foods—potato soup was a favorite; she also would mix hamburger and eggs together," Virginia said. "Her cooking was pretty sparse when she was living up at the lake. It wasn't for lack of electricity; she had it. She just fixed simple things, but well.

"Round steak pounded flat was a real treat. Once when we were visiting with my father, he sat there eating his steak and she kept asking him to eat more, and he took more just to make her happy. But really, he was full and he was slipping the steak into his pocket. She finally saw him doing it, and she was so mad. She said, 'here I am sitting in front of you and I don't have enough to eat and you are putting your steak in your pocket!' "

Besides her garden, travel was her passion.

"She travelled a lot. She said she'd been around the world several times. Her favorite place was New Zealand. She said there were a lot of people there who were horticulturists. She liked to travel so much. She traveled every chance she got, and she particularly liked cruises," Virginia said. "She would save as much money as she could so she could go traveling."

And yet, a visitor to her home would not have suspected she was well-off.

"She had so many quirks," Virginia Hill said. "She was an eccentric dresser; she didn't really worry too much about fashion in her everyday attire. When she lived at Squaw Lake, she would go around town in old ski pants. She had a huge diamond ring that she got from Sam Hill. But she wouldn't wear it. Instead, she had a phony one made just the same size, and she would wear it. She wouldn't throw out a pair of socks. She would just keep darning them."

Despite her frugality, or more likely because of it, she could afford to go south most winters. Her usual first stop was Grand Forks, where she would spend a month or more with her sister, Frances, and her family. Frances's son, Theron R. "Rod" Thoms, who lived in East Grand Forks until 2009, when he retired and moved to Colorado, remembers his aunt's cabin by the lake and her annual fall visits.

"She was tough," he said. "When you worked for her, you *worked*. I would spend a week up there most summers, and she had me filling holes in her road, hoeing the garden. I worked my butt off. Sam had a complete set of Hardy Boys books, and Mona didn't like me reading them. If she caught me reading, rather than working, she would get mad."

He would see her again in the fall.

"She would close up her cabin and then spend four to six weeks with us on her way to California for the winter," Thoms said. "She did that every winter. I remember she drove a big DeSoto."

Sometimes Mona brought Sam, who was 12 years older than Rod. It was evident Mona and Sam had a prickly relationship, Thoms said. He remembers them having a particularly loud argument one year when Sam was a teen-ager.

Thoms's sister, Bonnie Evans, remembers Mona's annual visits as being like visits from royalty.

"Her annual visits were fraught with tension," said Evans, who left Grand Forks late in her teens, moved to California, and then eventually settled in British Columbia. "My father didn't like her visits. He was very much the patriarchal German and resented the way Mona took center stage and ordered everyone about, including him. During his fifties, my father was drinking heavily, and he and my mother fought about his drinking nearly every day. He could always shut up my mother by saying, 'you're no better than your sister.' She did not have a comeback for that."

Hobart "Tommy" Thoms and Mona had known each other since 1918 or 1919, when Frances met her future husband in Minneapolis. Frances was living with Mona at the time. Bonnie suspects that Mona and Tommy probably got along better than the arguments Bonnie witnessed suggest. "They were both passionate about flowers and they both loved to hunt," Bonnie said. "It was only in the heat of arguments about his drinking that my father would make his disparaging remarks."

Even so, Bonnie remembers asking herself, "what's wrong with Auntie Mo?"

"My mother and Mona were very close," she said. "I think my mother hero-worshiped her."

Frances was as passive as Mona was aggressive, Bonnie said. "My mother was very much a depressed housewife. Before they adopted me and my brother, she and my dad traveled, they went out. But because they had to wait so long for children, I think she tried to be the supermother."

Frances, Mona and their brother, John, did not have a mother, basically, because Esther spent long hours running the store.

"When I complained to my mother about her parenting, she would remind me of her past and tell me I should be happy that I had a mother," Bonnie said. "She tried to be an overachieving mom. She was very protective. My mother always was convinced I was sick; Mona had no time for illnesses. Once, when I really was sick, Mona insisted the cure for me was a nice bowl of fish head soup."

The soup was just a threat.

"I don't think she was really serious," Bonnie said. "It was more like she was showing off or being provocative. Mona liked being provocative. When I think about her, her mannerisms remind me of a 1930s romantic comedy—*The Thin Man* or something—sort of flirty and devil-may-care. This was incongruous in a woman in her middle 50s, but probably mannerisms picked up when she was younger."

Mona's reclusive, mysterious persona at Dunbar Lake is not the way Bonnie remembers her aunt.

"I think of her as very social and almost flamboyant, and certainly dressed to the nines when she visited us. Maybe that was a side she only showed on her travels," she said.

Another striking contrast between the sisters was Mona's liberal attitude toward societal norms. She was more accepting of Bonnie's difficult situation when her first marriage fell apart.

"My first husband was black, and we had two children. My parents disowned me," Bonnie said. "When we divorced, I wrote to them to see if they would help me. My mother wrote back and said, 'why would we want to help you? You need to get rid of those children and come home.' I was horrified and wrote back and said I couldn't imagine doing that. Later, Mona said to me, 'I told your mother that if you give up those children because of what she said to you, she won't get a dime from me in my will.' Mona tried to control everyone with money. That was how she was. When I first went to California, and my parents were trying to get me to come home, Mona wrote to me that she would leave me $10,000 in her will if I would."

Money defined Mona most of her adult life, first at Bonneville where she lived in a hilltop mansion and was the subject of intense gossip about her relationship with the iconic Sam Hill, and later at Dunbar Lake, where neighbors perceived her lifestyle as one of obvious wealth, pleasure travel, and ease—despite her obvious frugality and her penchant for labor in her garden. In large part, Mona defined herself by her money.

"Mona was always very careful to make sure that everyone understood she was an important person," Bonnie said. "When she visited, she would come with eight million suitcases, it seemed, and she would gesture for my father to carry them into the house, and then she would sit around and tell us about her travels. Mona intimidated my mother, who, at least when I knew her, was Mona's opposite in personality. At the same time, though, my mother was both proud of and competitive with her sister. Mona was rich, or so we thought, but my mother was married to a successful businessman and very much part of the social elite of Grand Forks."

CHAPTER 11

The Lonely Son

*B*Y ANY MEASURE, SAM BETTLE HILL HAD AN UNUSUAL CHILDHOOD. AS A BOY, HE WASN'T EXACTLY FORGOTTEN, AND HE WASN'T EXACTLY NEGLECTED, BUT CERTAINLY HE WAS NOT THE HIGHEST PRIORITY IN HIS mother's life, either. Mona's relationship with him seems to have been more of a long-term acquaintance marked by periods of acceptance and rejection. She sent him to expensive boarding schools, where he often spent holidays while she traveled. He rebelled fiercely as a teen-ager, once being sought by the police after he took her car without permission.

Hugo Ojanen was a boyhood friend of Sam. Today, Ojanen lives in Bloomington, Minnesota, but he grew up on the family farm near Squaw Lake. The Ojanen farm was about three-quarters of a mile east of Mona's home on Dunbar Lake.

"I wasn't that close to Sam; I was kind of a shy kid," Ojanen said in a 2008 interview, when he was 77. "Mona bought him a lot of comic books. If I had them now, I'd be rich."

Ojanen described Sam, who was about two years older, as aloof but not unfriendly. He had a golden lab named Blondie, and the three of them would play, often in the lake. Once they went out in a rowboat, Sam and Hugo in the boat and Blondie swimming behind.

"Mona came to the shore and called, 'Sam, Sam,' but he just kept on rowing," Ojanen said.

It was clear to him that Sam's relationship with his mother was strained. Ojanen knew, for example, that Mona sent Sam away to school. Sam probably only attended the local school at Squaw Lake one year, when he was very young, and for that year he moved into the town and lived with a family named Millard.

Sam's difficult relationship with his mother also was clear to his cousin, Bonnie Evans, who knew him well. They spent time together at the cabin on Dunbar Lake, where she learned to fear Mona but also to respect her.

Bonnie is convinced that Mona simply didn't know how to be a mother, preferring to be aloof and self-important.

"I think she was essentially a very selfish person," Bonnie said. "She wanted to live her life the way she wanted to—if Sam was in the way, then send him off to my mother's or to a boarding school. In that sense she was very masculine, more like what a man would be."

Despite a difficult childhood, though, Sam persevered, finished college and graduate school, and had a successful career. With Virginia, he owned a restaurant and then a bar in Minneapolis. Later he worked as a probation officer in Albuquerque and Southern California, and after that he was a family therapist, also in Southern California.

He grew to be a big man, like his father—over six feet tall and easily over 200 pounds. Also like his father, he had a big head—literally—and he was loud, funny, gregarious and, at times, profane.

"I never had a memory of my father until I was about 40," he said in a 1985 interview, when he was 57 years old. "I was taking part in a bioenergetics workshop, kicking a mattress, when all of the sudden I remembered sitting on my father's lap holding onto his lapel. He had a tweed suit on, and he smelled of soap. He had a lapel button. It was red; a croix de guerre. He wore it all the time. I was playing with his mustache, and he was smiling at me." Mona and little Sam left the Gorge house a month before his seventh birthday, and so that memory very well could have been from one of elder Sam's visits to the hilltop.

As for the Gorge house, the memories were less pleasant.

"I have very sad memories about that," he said. "We had servants—a Filipino cook, an Indian gardener, and a maid—but otherwise it was just my mother and myself in the house. I remember my room. It was huge, with a bed in the middle. It looked out toward the river; there was a tree outside the window. It was a deciduous tree because I remember the leaves would fall. I could look down on the [Army] engineers' cabins below. I envied all of their children because they belonged to someone. I belonged to no one. I had no relationship with my mother."

Sam said he recalled the landscaped grounds and a fish pond with koi in front of the house. Inside, there was a large living room, a spiral staircase to the second floor, and a table in the dining room that could seat 12. The table, and a matching hutch, had been custom-made by a company in Michigan based on a sketch Mona brought back from a trip she made to Europe before Sam was born. The originals were in a monastery in France.

"There was an old hermit who lived on our land in a shack in the woods," Sam said. "I used to go and visit him, and that was a big thrill of my life. My mother let him live on our land. He used to walk along the road with me, and he'd sing 'Jesus Loves Me.' We'd part where the road split, and I would go up the hill to my house."

Mona was a mystery to her son all his life. In September 1985, she had been dead nearly four-and-a-half years, and Sam still could not comprehend her, other than to say simply: "My mother didn't want to be a mother; it was lonely in that house." His awkward, difficult relationship with his mother, and the lack of any father figure during his childhood, probably contributed to a personality disorder, his wife, Virginia, would say later. "He could be cruel toward people, but then he could be very loving and kind. People would refer to him as a big teddy bear," she said.

Like his mother and his famous father, Sam was a difficult person at times, and at other times loving and empathetic. With the possible exception of his mother, no one knew Sam better than Virginia. They met in 1950 at the University of Minnesota, where they were students.

"When I met him, I was already engaged to somebody else. I met him at school, in a class, and he would always come in late. He was the man about town, you know, staying up late and going to bars, and doing all this stuff. He was kind of a maverick against society. I was captivated," Virginia said. "He asked if he could copy my notes, and we got together to copy notes, and pretty soon we were an item and in love with each other."

It was a quick romance that led to marriage about six months after they met.

"I remember walking down the aisle saying, 'this is probably the dumbest thing I've ever done, because who is he?' We would go out on a Saturday night—this was later, after I'd had a couple of children—and women would come up to me and say, 'do you know him, Sam?' He'd flirt with everybody and all over the place, and I think that's kind of what old Sam Hill was like, too—gregarious, flirtatious. My Sam was not easy."

As newlyweds, Virginia and Sam settled in Minneapolis, where Sam worked as a collection officer for a clothing store and Virginia worked as a statistical analyst for Honeywell. But Sam was not happy, and Mona was the root of his angst.

"He was so angry with his mother; I think he was always angry with his mother, and afraid of her. I think he was more afraid than angry," Virginia said. "He told me so many times that when he was up there at the house in the Gorge, he wanted to die. He was really very unhappy. I imagine he was feeling isolated when they lived there."

From childhood on, Sam's relationship with his mother never was easy. Lonely, essentially fatherless as a child, a ward of boarding schools, he felt rejected. But he wasn't. Mona wanted him to be successful in life, and from time to time they would actually agree on things and work together.

"She was insistent that her son would graduate from college, and she paid for part of it," Virginia said. "Still, she could be pretty chincy with her money. I remember how mad I was when they decided—*they* decided—that he would go back to school to get his master's degree. That meant that I would have to go back to work full-time. If I would go back to work full-time, then she would give us $100 a month, but it was with *that* agreement. That's one of my regrets in life, that I had to work when my children were young. But that was the agreement *they* made."

The most contentious part of the relationship between mother and son was over his paternity, Virginia said. As a boy Sam believed Edgar Hill was his father because that is what Mona told him. But when Sam was about 20 his aunt Frances told him the truth.

"He was very angry with Mona for not telling him Sam really was his father, but later on he came to understand that she was trying to protect his name," Virginia said.

In fact, Mona never spoke the words "Sam Hill was your father" to her son, but when she was about 80 years old, she acknowledged the fact in so many words, or with a gesture of acquiescence to Sam's latest entreaty for the truth. In Sam's mind, that settled the question.

"Sam really never believed that Edgar was his father," Virginia Hill said. "He suspected it was Sam all along because Mona Bell kept a picture of him in her home. Sam knew that Edgar was Sam's cousin; when he was a teen-ager he went to Indiana and knocked on Edgar's door—I think he wanted a real father, you know—and confronted him. Edgar shut the door on him and said, 'get out of here; you aren't my son.' Edgar was not a nice man."

In fact, Mona long distrusted Edgar and believed that he had exploited Sam's trust in him as a manager of several of his businesses.

"She hated Edgar because she felt he had just ripped off Sam Hill," Virginia said. "He had been in charge of Sam Hill's finances. He was just terrible. He had been really sneaky."

Edgar died on Dec. 31, 1945, in Knightstown, Indiana, of injuries he sustained in an automobile accident in Oregon. For the next eight years, Mona fought a one-woman battle against the attorneys for his estate, trying to claim some part for her son. After all, Sam's birth certificate named Edgar as the father, even though she knew he was not. She confronted Edgar's attorneys with the document, and possibly others that named or implied his paternity. She also apparently had some records that she claimed proved Edgar had stolen from Sam, although those have long since disappeared. It wasn't exactly blackmail, but it was close.

Several letters in the Maryhill Museum archives demonstrate that Edgar's posthumous legal problems were known to the Hill family. In one letter, written in November 1946, Sam's cousin Daniel Hill, who lived in Seattle, wrote to Sam's son James in Boston about current events at Maryhill Museum. Daniel was the president of the museum's board of directors. Edgar had died, Daniel wrote, adding: "Your old friend Ed is having a hell of a time, or at least his executors are as a woman has brought a paternity suit against Ed's estate but I am glad I am not mixed up in the dirty mess."

The "dirty mess" may have been the subject of Mona's September 1946 meeting with Zola Brooks, the Maryhill Museum attorney. A letter of introduction from her old friend and attorney, Jay Bowerman, was cryptic in requesting the meeting. Mona and Brooks already were acquainted, however, as they had communicated periodically for the past 10 years to discuss the state of Sam's trust fund. The most recent of those meetings had been just the past July. The only thing of substance in Bowerman's letter was that he always had found Mona trustworthy, and so the reason for the meeting could have been more sensitive than simply another review of the trust fund status.

James Hill replied to Daniel Hill later that month, writing in part: "My memory of Edgar's second marriage is that it took place in Portland, Oregon, and that shortly afterwards he and his wife crossed the river to Vancouver, Washington, where a divorce was arranged, and that at that time a property settlement was made on her. He also told me that he was going to cut her and his son out of his will. Apparently this is what he did, and left his property to a certain relative; that is why she is bringing the suit on behalf of her son." James worried about the negative publicity the paternity suit might bring on the Hill family, but he also thought that such publicity was unlikely because Edgar was not well known in Indiana. James did not have a favorable opinion of Edgar: "He was always a cumbersome and awkward person to deal with, and I would also use the word precarious. That word could well describe the present situation." Daniel replied that the paternity suit had been dismissed in court, adding "Ed was precarious all right and I hope I have heard the last of him."

Virginia Hill recalls Mona telling her that she went after Edgar's estate both on behalf of her son and also because she was convinced Edgar had stolen from his cousin. "She went after Edgar's will," Virginia said. "She wanted to get even for what he had done to Sam Hill."

Mona also was an efficient, take-no-prisoners negotiator. She liked to win.

Virginia recalled, "She told me once, 'you just have to keep raising your voice until you get what you want. That's how you do it.' She was so proud of her ability to do that. This was how she was. She was an aggressive woman—not assertive, aggressive. Once I stopped being afraid of her, we got along very well. When I learned to have a voice and stand up to her, then she started respecting me. But she could come across as very harsh."

Virginia and Sam accompanied Mona to Indianapolis for a final confrontation in 1953. But Mona's plan was undone when her son inexplicably met privately with Edgar's heirs or attorneys and accepted their cash offer.

"I remember Mona Bell insisting that Sam was entitled to a portion of the estate," Virginia said. "It never went to trial because the other side didn't want it to. Sam talked to them, and when they offered him $28,000, he said, 'that's fine, I'll take it.' Mona Bell was very angry with him because he had settled for $28,000, and she wanted to get a lot more money than that. He didn't even talk to Mona Bell about it; he didn't even say he was going to take the offer. You can see why she was angry with him. Edgar's attorneys had been putting up with Mona Bell during the whole thing, and they were angry with her demands. She's the one who did all the writing with the attorneys; Sam hadn't done a thing."

But it was over. If Sam saw this as a competition with his mother, he had won. Sam and Virginia used part of the money to buy a new Plymouth sedan and put a down payment on a house in Minneapolis. But then Sam gambled away most of the rest of the money and they left Minnesota for their own safety. He didn't seem to care that the money came from Edgar's estate, or that Mona had fought Edgar's lawyers on his behalf.

"It was like he wanted to get rid of it, like he was ashamed of it," Virginia said.

His unhappiness was at the root of his gambling problem. At the time, Virginia and Sam had three young children. Sam's gambling was a threat not only to their domestic relations, but possibly to their lives.

"There was a group of really rough people—literally, the Mafia— who were involved, and he would be out all night. He was playing with fire. I decided I was going to leave the relationship, but then I told him that if he got psychotherapy, that would help," she said.

He did, and the diagnosis was not encouraging: Depression and an anti-social personality. However, he was not always depressed. "He could be very wonderful, and very brilliant, and very thoughtful—like his mama," Virginia said. The therapy helped, and Sam did better for awhile. The couple purchased a bar and restaurant. Virginia did the cooking.

But then Sam's gambling intensified again and, Virginia said, "we had to get out of town, basically. I would get these threatening phone calls at night, and we had three children, you know."

The West was sufficiently far away, and so Sam answered an advertisement by the State of New Mexico to pay for graduate school in exchange for working for the Department of Social Services. Virginia and Sam had driven through New Mexico on a vacation in 1953 and, remembering how much they liked the state, they moved to Albuquerque and stayed for about a year. They moved to Los Angeles in 1955, where Sam had been accepted in the graduate school at the University of Southern California.

"I didn't like the idea of LA, but I liked the idea of no snow," Virginia said.

After a year at USC, Sam left school to work for the county as a probation officer rather than return to Albuquerque. This meant he had to pay for the schooling, but he liked being a probation officer. Virginia thinks the work appealed to him because of his maverick streak—he liked being around bad guys. Sam remained interested in finishing his graduate work, and Virginia also wanted to pursue an advanced degree. So in the early 1960s, the couple moved north so Sam could attend the University of California at Berkeley, where he earned a Master's Degree in social work. Virginia taught school while Sam was at Berkeley, and then eventually got her own master's degree in social work.

Together, they opened a counseling service in Lancaster, and eventually moved to Venice. Virginia and Sam had three children: Patricia Jean, born in 1952; Paula Rae, born in 1953; and Sam Bettle, born in 1955 and named after his father. Patricia is deceased, Sam lives in the Los Angeles area, and Paula lives near Sacramento.

Paula remembers Mona mainly as an elderly woman who was slipping into dementia. She also remembers some less-than-pleasant holidays at home.

"She tortured dad when he was a kid, and so I guess he felt he had to torture us," she said. She did not elaborate.

CHAPTER 12

The California Transplant

*D*ESPITE HER LOVE FOR DUNBAR LAKE AND THE MINNESOTA WOODS, MONA EVENTUALLY TIRED OF LIVING THERE AND IN 1953 PACKED UP AND MOVED PERMANENTLY TO CALIFORNIA, SETTLING IN RIVERSIDE. THERE WAS NO apparent reason for the move other than she had visited the area, liked it, and decided to move. Perhaps she'd had enough Minnesota winters.

Mona sold the property to Forrest and Sylvia Cox in September 1954, for $11,000. She sold the property on contract, meaning that she retained ownership while the Coxes made payments. In essence, she was the bank.

The contract allowed the Coxes to cut 10,000 board feet of lumber from trees on the property to build a house. They did so, building on the foundation of the original cabin that had been destroyed by fire.[81] The contract stipulated that the Coxes would pay Mona $150 per month, or more if they chose, until they had paid a total of at least $5,500, at which point Mona would provide a warranty deed for the property and the Coxes would take out a mortgage for the remaining balance. Two years later, in September 1956, the sale was finalized according to the terms of the contract.

While the contract allowed the Coxes to cut trees to make lumber for their new home, the contract didn't say anything about the trees on the rest of the property, which was heavily wooded with old-growth pine and spruce. David Adams, who owns the home today with his wife, Marilyn, speculates that the Coxes wanted Mona's land for its timber value, and in fact cut hundreds of trees over time.

"From my deer stand I counted 1,500 stumps, some of them three and four feet across," he said.

There still are some trees on the property that Adams guesses are 200 years old—huge, beautiful, old trees—but most of the forest that stood when Mona lived there is gone. Adams said he heard from his family that at some point Mona tried to stop the Coxes from cutting so many trees, but having sold the property, there was nothing she could do.

"She really loved the trees," Adams said. Over time, the Coxes cut more than 1.5 million board feet of lumber from the property, he said.

In Riverside, Mona built a house, and like her homes at Bonneville and Dunbar Lake, it soon became a showplace for her flowers. The house was surrounded by raised beds—with boiled dirt. She had a large greenhouse where she worked to perfect a pink hybrid lily—pink was a difficult color to produce in lilies. In 1959, she traveled to New Zealand where she consulted with two lily experts.

In April 1960, her gardens were featured on the annual Riverside County Flower Show tour. An article about her gardens and lilies was printed in the Riverside newspaper. She evidently mailed a copy of that article to a contact in New Zealand. A follow-up article in the Riverside paper mentioned that the first one was read to members of the Auckland Lily Society.

She had no boyfriend in Riverside, at least none that she talked about, but she did have many friends. She was well-known in the city's gardening circles, and her abilities with flowers gave her a sort of rock-star status among local horticulturists. The Riverside (California) *Press-Enterprise* newspaper reported on Mona Bell several times in this regard.

Another time, she grabbed the pen from the hand of an interviewer, George Ringwald, a columnist for the same newspaper. Mona's home was on a cul-de-sac called Suffield Road. But this caused some confusion with the city's emergency services because Riverside also had a Sheffield Road. In 1968, city officials decided to rename Suffield and asked the people who lived there for suggestions. One suggested Mona Bell Court, and the others all agreed. Mona was traveling out of the country when the renaming occurred, and she returned to find her name on her street, a name it bears to this day.

The renaming drew Ringwald's attention, and he paid a visit to the Mona Bell of Mona Bell Court. He was smitten, he would later recall. At one point during the interview, Mona stopped talking in mid-sentence and grabbed the pen from his hand.[82] Newspaper people don't need to take notes, she declared. And she kept the pen.

Nearly 20 years later Ringwald, then retired in Eureka, California, recalled her "stern eye" and aversion to publicity. "Was she the one who grabbed away my pen at one point while I was busily scribbling notes? Sounds like it might have been," he wrote in a letter.[83]

At the time he wrote the column, Ringwald did not know that Mona had a son by Sam Hill—in fact, his 1968 column does not mention any children. In the 1985 letter, though, he suggested that might explain what he called Mona's "reluctance to get into print:"

> "... maybe it was because she'd gotten enough attention from the press in her day as the mistress of Sam Hill. In a sense, I suppose she was right in referring to him as a 'distant relation.' Wish I'd known about that connection at the time, although I don't suppose we'd have used it anyhow, given the Press-Enterprise's status in the community as a family newspaper." [84]

In fact, the press either ignored or never understood her true relationship with Sam. Mona always was portrayed as a distant relation of Sam or as the widow of Sam's cousin. That's how she wanted it, and she usually got what she wanted.

Other than her affiliation with local horticulture societies and the renamed street, she did not attract attention to herself during the nearly 30 years she lived in Riverside. She continued her frequent travels and displayed many collectibles brought home from exotic places. In 1958 she took her aging Africa films, now 23 years old, to film archivists at Walt Disney Studios to see if the images could be restored. But unfortunately, the low-quality stock had become so brittle that restoration was not possible.

Mona visited Sam and Virginia periodically, and she enjoyed spending time with her grandchildren, particularly Sam Bettle Hill, who was named after his father. Virginia says Mona saw him as "the son she never had."

While she was wealthy, she continued to be frugal to a fault.

"When we would go to her house to eat when the children were small she always would use paper napkins. We would use them for breakfast, and then after we had eaten we would fold them and put them on top of the refrigerator and use them again for lunch, and then for dinner. After she died, I went to her home to clean things up and found that she saved everything. I mean cottage cheese containers, everything."

She could laugh at herself over her lack of fashion sense, too.

"She liked to tell the story about how, when she was older, her son told her she needed to get a bra," Virginia said. "She said she hadn't realized she was sagging."

Five or six years before she died, Mona sold her home in Riverside and moved to a smaller, two-bedroom home adjacent to the Cherry Hills Country Club, today known as the California Golf and Art Country Club, in Sun City, California, about 30 miles south. For the last few years of her life, she had increasing problems. Her memory began to fade, and she suffered the onset of what must have been age-related dementia. She became introverted, anxious, and distrustful. Increasingly, she felt abandoned, as she wrote to her niece, Bonnie Evans, in April 1975. Mona's sister, Frances, who was Bonnie's mother, had died. "So sorry to hear of your loss, but I know you will never be sorry of all the pleasure and comfort you have given to your dear mother who loves you so much," she wrote. She offered her home to any of Bonnie's friends who might travel through the area, but added, "I could furnish them with bed and food while they were here but no service. At 85 I can't take care of myself, and no help available." She enclosed a check for $100, adding "I hope that will help a little."

Virginia and Sam, who lived about 100 miles to the northwest in Venice, could not check on her every day so they arranged for a caretaker to visit her on a regular basis. Even though Mona complained about having no one to help her, she refused to move to an assisted-care facility.

But the arrangement did not last.

"She aimed her gun, a revolver, at the caregiver and said she had to leave; then she called the police and said she was all by herself and no one would take care of her," Virginia said. "I told her that was the end and she would have to go into a home."

Mona balked at this, of course, but she had no choice.

"I always have to laugh; Mona Bell could be very difficult," Virginia said. "Sam wanted to get power of attorney for her when we saw her mind was starting to go. To do that we had to go to a mental health institution for an evaluation. She and I were sitting together in the evaluation room, and I can still see the scene very clearly. She was very proper, always. If she were here right now, she would be sitting up very straight. She had beautiful white hair. She and Sam had a lot of difficulties; he would get very nervous around her. He brought in a form for her to sign. I'll never forget; she had her old glasses on, and she looked down at the form and said, very slowly, 'S. B. Hill. What does that stand for, Son of a Bitch?' I fell off the bed laughing. She knew exactly what was going on, but she signed it. In fact, the way she said it, very slowly as if it were staged, made me think that she had said that very thing before. I wonder if it was a joke that she and old Sam had shared. It sounded like something she had said many times before."

She lived at the nursing home no more than six months before she died. It was a difficult time for her family because she was sedated to control her dementia.

Virginia recalled their last visit:

"Several months before she died, I told her, 'Mona Bell we're going to get the whole family together to see you, everybody will be here.' We did, it was in May."

Mona died shortly after the reunion, on June 1, 1981. She was 91 years old.

Mona's funeral was in a chapel at the Forest Lawn Hollywood Hills Cemetery, where she is buried.[85] "There weren't many people, mainly just the family," Virginia said. "We had her dressed in pastels, which she loved. I remember picking out something like "Rock of Ages," because she really liked the old hymns."

"She died one day into the month of June. I think she would have been proud that she lived long enough to get that last Social Security check," Virginia said.

CHAPTER 13

Life After Death

*M*ONA'S PARTING SHOT AT HER SON CAME AFTER SHE DIED.
WITHOUT TELLING SAM, MONA HAD NAMED A TRUST OFFICER
OF A RIVERSIDE BANK AS HER SUCCESSOR TRUSTEE. SAM WAS
surprised and hurt, and, of course, did not trust the man. Sam thought
he had stolen things from Mona's house but could not prove it.

While cleaning out the house in preparation for selling it, Sam found
a number of bearer bonds, which he took. Mona's estate at the end was
worth about $500,000. With this inheritance and the continuing checks
from the trust, "he didn't do much of anything after that," Virginia said.
He did not have access to the principal amount of the trust. Way back
in 1928, his father intended that the principal would go to Maryhill, and
not until Sam the son died. So the monthly checks continued to arrive,
and Sam continued to complain, as he had for years when the checks
had gone to his mother, that they were small—$200 to $250 per month.

Six years later, in 1987, Virginia and Sam divorced, and ten years
after that Sam died after a lengthy illness. He was 69 years old.

Virginia's memories of Sam are mixed—sometimes the loving
husband and doting father, other times angry and emotionally distant.
She blames his dark side on the lifelong friction with his mother, an
anger he never fully resolved.

"He could never let go of the past," she said. "He was in therapy
a lot over the years, but he just could not let go. It became a sort of
romantic thing with him to tell people how bad his childhood was. He
seemed to enjoy going over and over the dark side of his life. He denied
being depressed about it until late in his life. He was crippled by it,
and he did not want to be uncrippled. But at the same time, he was
brilliant and could be wonderful."

Virginia doesn't blame Mona, and, in fact, deeply admires her.

"She was brilliant, too. She had a presence. She was tall and
stately, and she just was not cut out to be a mother. She was a woman
alone, and she was OK with it," Virginia said. "She was such a strong

and proud woman, and she wasn't afraid to go any place or do anything on her own."

Today Mona's hilltop in the Columbia River Gorge is a mess of vines, fallen logs, overgrown bushes and a few remnants of the noble mansion that once stood there. The noise of the traffic on Interstate 84 below to the south, and the rumblings of the frequent trains on the Union Pacific tracks to the north echo in the shadowy recesses among the tall firs and pines that remain. Several trees are perhaps five feet across at the base; one of these giants is slowly pushing over the remains of a low wall of stones that, by its position in relation to the remains of the mansion, evidently once bordered the driveway.

It is possible to imagine where the fish pond was, where the irrigation pipes ran, where the sun room off the kitchen faced, the master bedroom balcony directly above. From that viewpoint, there would have been a stunning vista to the west, as it is even today: the broad river below Bonneville Dam frames a postcard view of Beacon Rock. There is wildlife on the hill, as there must have been when Mona lived there—deer, and a variety of birds, including raptors and song birds.

It is a shame that such a magnificent structure could not have been preserved in such a unique place. But given the need for speed on the freeway, and the limited potential alignments for the widened roadway and the relocated railroad tracks, Mona's mansion was the unfortunate victim of late-1950s economic development. The northeastern and southwestern extremes of the house literally would have been on the edges of the current hilltop, or hanging in mid air. Some different configuration of freeway and railroad likely would have been necessary to accommodate the structure. The expense would have been great, and apparently the mansion had no allies to argue for its preservation, at least none whose voices were strong enough to change the course of events. By the late 1950s, at any rate, the place was a wreck.

"It was all boarded up; it had been vacant for years, and we thought it was haunted," said Andrew DeBriae, who grew up at Bonneville Dam where his mother was a secretary in the project office and his father was a control room operator in the powerhouse. We kids used to scramble up that rock and play around the house."

DeBriae was born in 1952. Like his parents, he is a Corps employee at Bonneville Dam, where he is a structural crew foreman. He grew up in House No. 19 in the community of Corps of Engineers employees below the hill, which he knew as Bonny Rock. He was seven years old when the house came down.

"I don't remember it being that big, but I do remember it had a turret on the front and a big tile patio in the back," he said. "They blasted the south side of Bonny Rock for the freeway, and one day the house was just gone."

DeBriae collects photos of Bonneville Dam, including photos of its construction. He said some show Mona's house nestled in the trees atop Bonny Rock.

Meanwhile, Mona's memory lives on with her family and the things she left to them. Mona's dining room table, chairs, and hutch from the mansion are in Virginia Hill's dining room at her home in the Los Angeles area.

"They will stay in our family forever," she said.

An unusual piece of furniture from the mansion, an upright piano converted to a desk, is in the Sacramento-area home of Virginia's daughter, Paula, as are some other pieces of Mona's furniture. Virginia's son, Sam, has the large photo of his grandfather, in its original frame backed with purple velvet, that Mona proudly displayed in all the places she lived. Virginia also has jewelry, artwork, and souvenirs that Mona brought back from her world travels, including a stunning silk kimono in hues of cream, orange, and black. It hangs on a wall of her dining room. There is also fine silver jewelry from Mexico, carved wooden figurines that have a southeast Asian appearance, and knives, spears, and a shield from Africa that seems to have been made from layers of giant banana leaves or something similar. Virginia also has Mona's yellow crystal wine glasses. Mona liked yellow.

There is very little about Mona in the Maryhill Museum of Art. This is not unusual, as there is very little about any of Sam Hill's three mistresses in the museum, other than a few photos and records of the trusts he established for the benefit of their children and, ultimately, the museum. Sam kept his personal life, and these relationships, secret as much as he was able. Mona did the same. Her son said in 1985 that

Mona kept all of her correspondence with Sam, including their love letters, but burned it all sometime late in her life.

In the Sam Hill Room at the Maryhill Museum, pictures of Sam's three children by his mistresses hang on a wall. The photo of Sam B. Hill was taken when he was about five years old. Virginia knows that photo and believes it was taken at one of the boarding schools, and probably with Sam on horseback. He liked horses.

Despite the minimal attention at the museum and Mona's reticence about her relationship with Sam, Mona's descendants find her fascinating and are proud of their connection to Sam Hill. They all have visited Maryhill and plan to make future trips. Virginia likes to tell the story about her granddaughter, Samantha, daughter of Virginia's son Sam and thus the youngest "Sam" Hill, wowing her elementary school classmates with a report about her famous great-grandfather. "She has Mona in her," Virginia said proudly. "She loves to perform."

Virginia says she still feels Mona's presence from time to time—when she sits at the dining room table or sees her handwriting on one of the recipe cards she inherited, for example. It's been like that ever since she died, as if she remains with the family in spirit as well as in memory. Virginia laughs when she recalls one incident of Mona's apparent continuing presence, an incident involving the photo of the teen-aged Mona who made herself pretty to win a bet.

"We were living in Venice when our daughter, Paula, got married. We had the reception at our house, and the reception line wound through the living room where we were standing—right in front of the photo. I turned to Sam and said, 'it's too bad Mona Bell isn't here.' And at that very instant, the photo fell off the wall. It had never fallen before!"

Notes

Introduction: In Search of Mona Bell Hill

[1] John Tuhy's book, *Sam Hill: The Prince of Castle Nowhere*, was published by Timber Press, Portland, in 1983. He writes about Mona Bell on pages 286-289.

[2] I interviewed Sam B. Hill at the Marriott Downtown Hotel, Portland, Oregon, on Sept. 12, 1985. Sam was on his way to the Maryhill Museum to attend a meeting of the board of directors. He was not a member of the Board. This was our only face-to-face meeting.

Chapter 1: Mona Bell

[3] Records of Mona's attendance at the University of North Dakota were supplied by Monty E. Nielson, Acting Director, Office of Admissions and Records, in a letter to me dated Nov. 29, 1985.

[4] Background about Buffalo Bill's Wild West, and Mona's possible employment, was provided by Lynn J. Houze, Curatorial Assistant, Buffalo Bill Museum, Cody, Wyoming. This was in two e-mails, dated August 7, and 11, 2003.

[5] Sam and Virginia Hill, husband and wife, were not interviewed at the same time. Sam spoke about his memories of his mother during our interview in Portland in 1985 (see note 2 above); Virginia Hill recalled Mona in interviews in 2007 at her home and office in the Los Angeles area. Sam and Virginia were divorced in 1987.

Chapter 2: Sam Hill

[6] Lockley, Fred. History of the Columbia River Valley from The Dalles to the Sea. S.J. Claril Publishing Co., Chicago, 1928.

[7] The AB stands for Artium Baccalaureus. It is the equivalent of a modern-day Bachelor of Arts degree.

[8] Sam's life is well-chronicled in John E. Tuhy's 1983 biography, *Sam Hill: The Prince of Castle Nowhere,* See note 1 above.

[9] Both John Tuhy and Albro Martin note in their biographies of Sam Hill and James J. Hill, respectively, that the engagement of Sam and Mary was brief. Tuhy cites a later telegram from Sam to Mary that pinpoints the date August 13, 1887, without any specific context. This may have been the date of their engagement, but that is not clear. At any rate, the actual date was not recorded publicly.

[10] Ironically, before Sam began working for one of his future father-in-law's railroads, he fought the St. Paul, Minneapolis & Manitoba line in court for 10 years on behalf of a competitor railroad over a matter of track location, and won. Probably it was this successful litigation, in

combination with the many personal injury cases he also won against J.J.'s lines, that convinced him to hire Sam.

[11] Martin, Albro. *James. J. Hill and the opening of the Northwest.* New York: Oxford University Press, 1976. Page 354.

[12] Tuhy, Page 230, writes that Sam told his Seattle friend Paul Douglas about meeting Marie in 1893 with a letter of introduction from Queen Victoria, her grandmother. But there is no proof the two met that year, and in fact it may have been much later. For example, Tuhy also cites a letter to Marie in 1917 in which Sam notes that she "fought the good fight" through "the sufferings" of her country, presumably those of World War I. The tenor of the letter, while quite formal, suggests the two were personally acquainted by then.

[13] Tuhy, Page 50.

[14] Martin, Page 529.

[15] After Mamie and the children left Seattle, the children returned West for periodic visits, but Mamie never did. One interesting record of such a trip is preserved in the guest books of the Crown Point Chalet, a roadhouse that once stood on the Columbia River Highway near Crown Point on the Oregon side of the Columbia River Gorge. Daughter Mary signed the guestbook in July 1915 and listed her home as Washington, D.C. A week earlier, Sam had signed the same guestbook and gave his address as Maryhill.

[16] Tuhy, Page 81.

Chapter 3: A Woman Alone
[17] Records of the International Correspondence Schools of Scranton, PA, have been archived at the University of Scranton. A finding aid to the university's holdings is located at: http://academic.scranton.edu/department/wml/icsfinding.html

[18] Erin Foley, Archivist, Circus World Museum Library, Baraboo, Wisconsin, provided a copy of the *Billboard* article in an e-mail dated Sept. 12, 2003.

[19] The Hill family's account that Sam married Mona and Edgar is disputed by Judith St. Martin, an historian who has catalogued the Sam Hill archives at Maryhill Museum. "This just doesn't sound like something Sam would do," she said.

[20] Sam was one of three wealthy Quakers in Seattle who together donated about $19,000 to pay for construction of the first building for the Seattle Monthly Meeting, also known as the Friends Memorial Church, in 1907. The building was at 23rd and Spruce and replaced the large tent the Friends had been using for meetings at another location. Attendance records have not survived from those early days, but the

pastor of the modern successor congregation, Lorraine Watson of the North Seattle Friends Church, wrote in an October 2007 e-mail: "It is clear that the church enjoyed a good relationship with him during those early years. We are grateful to Sam Hill and his friends for the significant boost they gave to the congregation by providing them with a building in those early days."

Chapter 4: The Mansion Atop Bonneville Rock

[21] Bureau of Land Management, General Land Office Records for the Oregon City, Oregon, Land Office. Issue Date: March 27, 1866, Doc. No. 1620, Accession/Serial No. OROCAA 048584.

[22] Bureau of Land Management, General Land Office Records for the Oregon City, Oregon, Land Office. Issue Date Oct. 8, 1901, Doc. No. 6309, Accession/Serial No. OROCAA 049242.

[23] Records of Multnomah County, Oregon, Deed Book 682, Page 207. The two cousins were Edgar, who lived in Seattle and who later would be nominally married to Mona by Sam when she became pregnant with Sam's baby; and David, who lived at Columbus, Washington, the town nearest to Sam's planned community of Maryhill, and who managed Sam's business affairs there.

[24] Telegrams to Sam in April 1910 from either Montague or Potter or both, five messages in all, regard an upcoming meeting in Portland to "negotiate with L.A. bondholders" and also refer to a hearing in Tacoma on May 6. This was 13 months after Sam bought the telephone company. There are no other details in the telegrams, and it is not clear whether the subject was telephone company bonds or some other company's bonds. Regardless, Potter and Montague clearly were business associates of Sam. The telegrams are in the Sam Hill Collection at the Maryhill Museum.

[25] Records of Multnomah County, Oregon, Deed Book 745, Page 104. Officially, the parcel is described as the southwest quarter of the southeast quarter of Section 21, Township 2 North, Range 7 East of the Willamette Meridian.

[26] Tuhy, page 124-125.

[27] Records of Multnomah County, Oregon, Deed Book 168, Page 498. This deed, dated April 4, 1932, states that it was filed to correct an error—that U.S. Trust intended to transfer the property to Samuel Hill, Inc., on Oct. 1, 1928, but that a deed filed on that date for several parcels apparently omitted the Gorge property "through error." The April 1932 deed states that "the covenants of warranty herein are made as of October 1, 1928."

[28] Records of Multnomah County, Oregon, Deed Book 143, Page 350.

[29] Bonneville, the place and the dam, were named for Capt. Benjamin

Louis Eulalie De Bonneville of the U.S. Army, who was born in France, emigrated to the United States, graduated from West Point, and had an exciting career as an officer, fur trapper, and western explorer. His exploits were chronicled by Washington Irving in *"The Adventures of Captain Bonneville"*, which tells about Bonneville's western exploration of 1832-35.

[30] The water right was proven and certified by a document recorded in the State Record of Water Rights Certificates three years later, on Oct. 29, 1931 (State of Oregon to Edith M. Bell Hill. Oct. 29, 1931. Certificate of proof of water right. Oregon Department of Water Resources, State Record of Water Right Certificates, Volume 9, Page 9,223). From that day, the water right was hers for 50 years.

[31] Henry Kunowski to John Harrison, e-mail, November 8, 2007.

[32] No record of the marriage or divorce of Mona Bell and Edgar Hill could be found in the archives of King, Pierce, Snohomish, Whatcom, or Klickitat counties, Washington, or Multnomah County, Oregon, all likely places where the wedding could have occurred and a divorce recorded.

[33] Correspondence, File No. OM-5, Mrs. E. Bell Hill, Records of the Real Estate Office, Portland District, U.S. Army Corps of Engineers, National Archives and Records Administration, Pacific Alaska Region, Seattle.

[34] I interviewed Harold Bailey by telephone in the fall of 1985.

[35] Plotts, Lois D. *Maryhill, Sam Hill and Me.* Copyright Lois Davis Plotts, Vancouver, Washington, 1978. Pages 80-82.

[36] Fisher, Lorena S. 1991. *The Bonneville Dream.* Copyright Lorena Fisher, Lake Oswego, Oregon.

[37] Tuhy, Page 277.

[38] Seattle Post-Intelligencer. February 27, 1931, Page 1.

[39] The United States Trust Company, Sam Hill's investment firm, declared a trust on December 15, 1928, with $60,000 par value of its own bonds with instructions that the interest would be paid to Mona Bell Hill as guardian of young Sam as long as he lived. According to the trust document, if he died before she did, the interest would be paid to her, and if she died before he legally was an adult, the interest would be paid to his designated guardian until he was an adult, and after that to him until he died. The trust did not stipulate to whom the interest should be paid if young Sam outlived his mother. But the declaration did make clear that the trust would transfer to Maryhill Museum when both were dead "subject to the payment of the income as herein set forth." *Seattle-First National Bank as Trustee vs. Mrs. E. Bell Hill, Samuel Hill and Maryhill Museum of Fine Arts.* Decree. Cause No. 290240, King County Superior Court, Seattle, January 1937. When Mona died, the interest was paid to Sam, and when he died, the principal amount reverted to the museum.

[40] It took another 10 years and more litigation—until September 1946—for the United States Trust Company, the executor, to settle Sam's complicated estate.

Chapter 5: Bonneville Dam
[41] Willingham, William J. 1997. *Water Power in the 'Wilderness:' The History of Bonneville Lock and Dam.* Portland: U.S. Army Corps of Engineers. Pages 1-6.

Chapter 6: The Battle
[42] $25,600 and $100,000 in 1934 had the buying power of $404,428 and $1,579,798 respectively in 2008, calculated in terms of changes in the Consumer Price Index. www.bls.gov, accessed March 31, 2008.

[43] Records pertaining to the real estate transactions and condemnation proceedings are held by the National Records and Archives Administration, Seattle, and located in two files: 1) Records Group 21, Box 469, No. 18790; and 2) Portland District, U.S. Army Corps of Engineers, Correspondence File No. OM-5, Box 6/20, "Mrs. E. Bell Hill." Certain real estate records also are held by the Information Management Office of the Corps of Engineers in the Portland District Headquarters, Portland, Oregon, in Records Group OM-5/14.7.

[44] *The Morning Oregonian*, Nov. 6, 1934.

[45] In retirement, Governor Meier lived at Menucha, but it would be a short retirement as he died in 1937 at the age of 63.

[46] Adjusted for inflation, $78,661.50 in 1935 dollars is the same as $1,215,480.94 in 2008 dollars. www.bls.gov, accessed March 26, 2008. On the same day, the government paid $526.22 into the registry of the court to satisfy the verdict in favor of West Coast Power Company for the loss of its right-of-way across Mona's property. The jury awarded West Coast $485. Interest at 6 percent from Feb. 9, 1934, totaled $41.22.

[47] The record does not indicate whether Bowerman claimed any part of the award for his own fees.

Chapter 7: Private Showplace to Public Derelict
[48] Willingham, William. 1997. *"Water Power in the 'Wilderness: The History of Bonneville Lock and Dam."* Portland. U.S. Army Corps of Engineers. Page 25.

[49] Ibid. Page 26.

[50] Sam Hill quoted by Sam Lancaster in Fred Lockley's interview with Lancaster in *History of the Columbia Valley from The Dalles to the Sea*, S.J. Claril Publishing Co., 1928.

[51] Baldock, R.H. 1936. *The Plans for the Improvement of the Columbia River Highway in the Columbia River Gorge.* Unpublished report for presentation to the Oregon State Highway Commission, April, 1936.

Archives of the Oregon Department of Transportation, Salem.

[52] *The Oregonian*, Nov. 11, 1956, Page 1.

[53] The tunnel remains in use today, carrying the eastbound lanes of Interstate 84. The tunnel begins a half-mile east of Mona's hilltop.

[54] J.M. Devers to R.H. Baldock. April 12, 1937. Archives of the Oregon Department of Transportation, Salem.

[55] In 1931 the Oregon State Parks Commission authorized the purchase of 25 acres immediately west of Mona's property. This flat land along the river included the site of Camp Get-A-Way, which had been built by Samuel Lancaster, Sam Hill's partner in the development of the Columbia River Highway. The camp burned to the ground in the late 1920s. Lancaster decided it would be too expensive to rebuild and sold the property to W.A. Alcorn, who sold it to the parks commission. Two years later, though, in 1933, the War Department announced it needed the property for the Bonneville Dam project, and the state deeded it to the government at no charge. Over time, the state regained most of the Lancaster/Alcorn property and, combined with additional acreage in the area created Bonneville State Park, which never was developed with visitor facilities.

[56] Devers to Baldock. April 7, 1938. Archives of the Oregon Department of Transportation, Salem.

[57] Samuel Boardman to J.M. Devers. September 15, 1938. Archives of the Oregon Department of Transportation, Salem.

[58] J.M. Devers to Lt. Col. Ralph A. Tudor. June 3, 1944. Archives of the Oregon Department of Transportation, Salem.

[59] E. Wilbur Barnes to J.M. Devers. January 15, 1945. Archives of the Oregon Department of Transportation, Salem.

[60] S.H. Boardman to J.M. Devers. January 18, 1946. Archives of the Oregon Department of Transportation, Salem.

[61] Foster Steele, Acting Supervisor, Mount Hood National Forest, to J.M. Devers. April 16, 1946. Archives of the Oregon Department of Transportation, Salem.

[62] Charles S. Cohn to Mount Hood Forest Supervisor. May 28, 1946. Archives of the Oregon Department of Transportation, Salem.

[63] C.H. Armstrong, State Parks Superintendent, to C.W. Enfield, Chief Counsel, State Highway Commission. Nov. 29, 1954. Archives of the Oregon Department of Transportation, Salem.

[64] F.A. Morgan, assistant attorney, to C. H. Armstrong, State Parks Superintendent. January 6, 1955. Archives of the Oregon Department of Transportation, Salem.

[65] Baldock wrote in *The Oregonian* for Dec. 8, 1954: "None of these tunnels ever should be reopened because of the danger to the people using the road, and an official would certainly assume a grave responsibility if he knowingly permitted traffic to be subjected to the positive danger involved." The Mitchell Point tunnel, at about milepost 58, remained in use until 1936, when the Tooth Rock Tunnel, at milepost 41 a half-mile east of Mona's hilltop, was opened, completing construction of an alternative route closer to the river. The Mitchell Point Tunnel finally was demolished in 1966 when the highway was widened and straightened in that area. The Oneonta Tunnel at the mouth of Oneonta Creek near milepost 34 was filled and abandoned in 1948 but dug out in 2006 and now is part of a trail along the old highway. Despite Baldock's admonishment, the Mosier Twin Tunnels, near milepost 68, remain in use—for pedestrians and bicyclists, however, not for vehicles. The tunnels today are part of the Historic Columbia River Highway State Trail, which is the old highway between Hood River and Mosier, a distance of just under five miles. Like the Oneonta Tunnel, the Mosier Twin Tunnels had been filled with rock and abandoned, but the debris was removed and the tunnels reopened for the trail in 1996; a visitor center opened in 2000. The tunnels have been reinforced, the windows in the rock that afford views of the river far below remain intact, and the experience of bicycling or walking through the tunnels recalls as close as possible the experience of tourists who marveled at the highway when it was new. At least once each summer, the trail is opened to vintage vehicles.

[66] Armstrong cites the date of the transfer as April 10, 1942, as does Samuel Boardman in his own history of the park written 13 years earlier, but there is no documentation to back that up in either account, and in fact the date contradicts other records in the state archives, noted earlier in this chapter, that the official date of the transfer was January 1, 1945.

[67] Armstrong does not say who bought the home.

[68] Armstrong, Chester H. *Oregon State Parks History, 1917-1963.*" Archives of the Oregon State Parks Commission, Salem.

[69] Boardman, Samuel H. *Bonneville: A Park of Destiny.* Oregon State Parks Commission, March 12, 1952. Archives of the Oregon State Parks and Recreation Department, Salem.

Chapter 8: Around the World
[70] San Francisco *Call Bulletin*, "Just Like a Woman!" Sept. 6, 1935 (page not indicated).

Chapter 9: The Savvy Investor
[71] John P. Garvin, attorney for Seattle-First National Bank, to Zola O. Brooks, attorney for Maryhill Museum. Dec. 30, 1936. Sam Hill

Collection, Maryhill Museum Archives.

[72] *Seattle-First National Bank vs. Mrs. E. Bell Hill, Samuel Hill, and Maryhill Museum of Fine Arts.* Plaintiff's complaint, King County Superior Court Docket No. 290240, May 28, 1936. Sam Hill Collection, Maryhill Museum Archives.

[73] John P. Garvin to Zola O. Brooks. October 6, 1936. Sam Hill Collection, Maryhill Museum Archives.

[74] Garvin to Brooks. Dec. 3, 1936. Sam Hill Collection, Maryhill Museum Archives.

[75] *Seattle-First National Bank vs. Mrs. E. Bell Hill, Samuel Hill, and Maryhill Museum of Fine Arts.* Plaintiff's complaint, King County Superior Court Docket No. 290240, January (day not noted) 1937. Sam Hill Collection, Maryhill Museum Archives.

[76] Jay Bowerman to Zola Brooks. September 17, 1946. Sam Hill Collection, Maryhill Museum Archives.

[77] David D. Ditzler, Assistant Trust Officer, to J.G. Scripps, Treasurer of the Maryhill Museum of Fine Arts. January 18, 1968. Sam Hill Collection, Maryhill Museum Archives.

Chapter 10: A Most Unusual Neighbor

[78] While Mona moved permanently to the lake in 1936, there is some evidence that she had at least visited the cabin before and perhaps during the time she lived in Portland and later in the Columbia River Gorge. The minutes of the Board of Supervisors of Good Hope Township, Itasca County, Minnesota, for March 24, 1928, include the following: "Board decided to, in order to give Miss Edith Mona Hill access to her place, rent roadway for this year threw [sic] J. Ronning's land at a compensation of five dollars." Thus, seven years before Esther Bell officially deeded the cabin and property to Mona, she already was known there as the owner or person-of-record of the cabin. Perhaps Esther and Henry bought it for Mona in the first place, or perhaps she had visited so many times as a young woman that she was the presumed owner and heir. At any rate the Township, and not Mona, paid to rent the road. There is one other interesting fact about the entry in the minutes of the Supervisors' meeting: Mona's last name is recorded as Hill, and this was in March, when she would have been about four months pregnant with her son, who would be born in August. The entry does not indicate whether Mona attended the supervisors' meeting, but it does at least suggest that her nominal marriage to Edgar occurred before March 1928. The mystery deepens, as well, as she is referred to as "Miss" Hill, not Mrs., yet Hill was her married name. Thus, she might have portrayed herself as divorced or widowed, as she would later, further complicating the question of when and whether Mona actually married and divorced Edgar Hill.

[79] Mona's unique cabin, however, is gone. It was struck by lightning on May 10, 1982, caught fire, and burned to the ground.

[80] Just what kind of car Mona drove is a matter of speculation. Another former neighbor, Hugo Ojanen, said she always drove DeSotos.

Chapter 12: The California Transplant

[81] In 2007, Marilyn Adams wrote: "That pine is still the interior walls and ceiling of our cabin. Some of the ceilings have been painted white to lighten the rooms, but the walls are all still pine (except the bathroom)." Marilyn Adams to John Harrison, e-mail dated Dec. 13, 2007.

[82] Riverside Press-Enterprise, "They named the street after her because they saw her as a character," Sept. 1, 1968.

[83] George B. Ringwald to John Harrison, Nov. 14, 1985.

[84] Ibid.

[85] Mona is buried in the Summerland section of the Forest Lawn Hollywood Hills Cemetery, Lot 6129, Space 2.